Key Concepts
in
American History

Federalism

Key Concepts
in
American History

Federalism

Darrell J. Kozlowski

Jennifer L. Weber, Ph.D.
General Editor
University of Kansas

CHELSEA HOUSE
PUBLISHERS
An imprint of Infobase Publishing

Key Concepts in American History: Federalism

DEVELOPED, DESIGNED, AND PRODUCED BY DWJ BOOKS LLC

Chelsea House
An imprint of Infobase Publishing
132 West 31st Street
New York NY 10001

Library of Congress Cataloging-in-Publication Data

Kozlowski, Darrell J.
   Federalism / Darrell J. Kozlowski ; Jennifer L. Weber, general editor.
      p. cm. – (Key concepts in American history)
   Includes bibliographical references and index.
   ISBN 978-1-60413-218-2 (hardcover)
1. Federal government–United States–History–Encyclopedias, Juvenile. 2. States' rights (American politics)–History–Encyclopedias, Juvenile. I. Weber, Jennifer L., 1962– II. Title.
   JK311.K69 2009
   320.4'049–dc22

                       2009025281

Cover printed by Bang Printing, Brainerd, MN
Book printed and bound by Bang Printing, Brainerd, MN
Date printed: May 2010
Printed in the United States of America

10 9 8 7 6 5 4 3 2 1

Acknowledgments
p. 1: Hall of Representatives, Washington, D.C./Bridgeman Art Library; pp. 13, 37, 47, 49, 56, 98, 102: The Granger Collection/New York; p. 67: U.S. Census Bureau, Public Information Office (PIO); p. 89: Joe Scherschel/National Geographic/Getty Images.

Contents

Viewpoints About Federalism

List of Illustrations

Photos

Maps

Reader's Guide
to Federalism

The list that follows is provided as an aid to readers in locating articles on the big topics or themes in American history and government. The Reader's Guide arranges all of the A to Z entries in *Key Concepts in American History: Federalism* according to these **5 key concepts** of the social studies curriculum: **Concepts and Ideas; Law and Legislation; People and Society; Principles of Government**; and **Social Movements**. Some articles appear in more than one category, helping readers to see the links between topics.

Concepts and Ideas
Albany Plan of Union (1754)
Block Grants
Direct Popular Election and Federalism
Electoral College System
Federalist System
Federalist, The
Loose Constructionist
New Federalism
Political Parties
Shared Powers
States' Rights
Strict Constructionist

Law and Legislation
Articles of Confederation (1781)
Block Grants
Census
Connecticut Compromise
Constitutional Convention
Direct Popular Election and Federalism
Elastic Clause
Electoral College System
Gibbons v. Ogden (1824)
Loose Constructionist
McCulloch v. Maryland (1819)
Political Parties
Reapportionment and Redistricting
Seventeenth Amendment (1913)
States' Rights
Strict Constructionist
Tenth Amendment (1791)
Virginia and Kentucky Resolutions
Voter Registration
Voting Rights Act (1965)

People and Society
Adams, John (1735–1826)
Calhoun, John C. (1782–1850)
Clay, Henry (1777–1852)
Direct Popular Election and Federalism
Electoral College System
Franklin, Benjamin (*see* Albany Plan of Union)
Hamilton, Alexander (1755–1804)
Henry, Patrick (1736–1799)
Jackson, Andrew (1767–1845)
Jefferson, Thomas (1743–1826)
Madison, James (*see* Constitutional Convention)
Marshall, John (1755–1835)
Nixon, Richard (1913–1994)
Political Parties
Reagan, Ronald (1911–2004)
Reapportionment and Redistricting
Shays, Daniel (*see* Shays's Rebellion)
Sherman, Roger (*see* Connecticut Compromise)
Voter Registration
Voting Rights Act (1965)
Washington, George (1732–1799)
Webster, Daniel (1782–1852)

Principles of Government
Albany Plan of Union (1754)
Articles of Confederation (1781)
Census
Connecticut Compromise

Constitutional Convention
Direct Popular Election and Federalism
Elastic Clause
Electoral College System
Federal City: Washington, D.C.
Federalist System
Federalist, The
Gibbons v. Ogden (1824)
Loose Constructionist
McCulloch v. Maryland (1819)
New Federalism
Political Parties
Reapportionment and Redistricting
Seventeenth Amendment (1913)
Shared Powers
States' Rights
Strict Constructionist
Tenth Amendment (1791)
Virginia and Kentucky Resolutions
Voter Registration
Voting Rights Act (1965)

Social Movements
Direct Popular Election and Federalism
Federalist System
Federalist, The
New Federalism
Shays's Rebellion
States' Rights
Virginia and Kentucky Resolutions
Voter Registration
Voting Rights Act (1965)
Whiskey Rebellion (1794)

Milestones in

Federalism is a system of government in which powers are shared among different levels of that government. It forms the basis of the government of the United States. An early idea for a **federalist** system can be traced back to 1754, when Benjamin Franklin first proposed the Albany Plan of Union. Through the years, political leaders have argued over which holds more power—the central government or the state governments.

The Union victory in the Civil War (1861–1865) ended the most serious debate about the issue. Yet, since the end of that war, many people continue to argue for a degree of states' rights. In the twentieth century, as the United States faced new foreign and domestic challenges, the power of the federal government increased significantly. In particular, the federal government has worked to guarantee equal rights for all Americans.

1754   Benjamin Franklin proposes the Albany Plan of Union.

1781   The Articles of Confederation are ratified by all 13 states.

1788   The U.S. Constitution is ratified by 9 of the 13 states.

1789   George Washington (1789–1797) is inaugurated as the first U.S. president.

1791   The First Bank of the United States is established.

1787   Federalist John Adams (1787–1801) is inaugurated as the second president of the United States.

1798   The Alien and Sedition Acts are passed; Virginia and Kentucky Resolutions (or Resolves) are written.

1801   Democratic-Republican Thomas Jefferson (1801–1809) is inaugurated as the third president; political power transfers peacefully from one party to another for the first time in American history.

1819   *McCulloch v. Maryland* establishes the supremacy of federal laws.

1824   *Gibbons v. Ogden* establishes national supremacy over interstate commerce.

1832   South Carolina threatens to nullify the federal Tariff of 1832; President Andrew Jackson (1829–1837) vetoes a bill renewing the Bank of the United States.

1833   Jackson orders all federal money withdrawn from the Bank of the United States.

1860   Abraham Lincoln (1861–1865) is elected the 16th president of the United States; South Carolina secedes from the Union.

1861   The Civil War begins.

1650 • 1700 • 1750 • 1800 • 1850 • 1900 • 1950 • 2000

Federalism (1789-Present)

1861 The Civil War begins.

1863 Lincoln issues the Emancipation Proclamation on January 1, freeing the slaves in lands under Confederate control.

1865 The Civil War ends, the Thirteenth Amendment to the U.S. Constitution, which officially ends slavery, is ratified.

1868 The Fourteenth Amendment to the U.S. Constitution, which defined citizenship and established that equal protection of the law is due to all citizens, is ratified.

1896 *Plessy v. Ferguson* establishes that "separate but equal" facilities for whites and blacks are constitutional.

1913 The Seventeenth Amendment to the U.S. Constitution, which gave citizens the right to directly elect U.S. senators, is ratified.

1954 *Brown v. Board of Education* declares segregation unconstitutional; the modern civil rights movement begins.

1964 The Civil Rights Act of 1964 is passed by Congress.

1965 The Voting Rights Act of 1965 guarantees the right to vote; it establishes federal responsibility for voting qualifications.

1969 Richard Nixon (1969–1974) is inaugurated as the 37th president of the United States; he promises to return more power to the states.

1974 Richard Nixon resigns the presidency as a result of the Watergate scandal.

1981 Ronald Reagan (1981–1989) is inaugurated as the 40th president; he promises New Federalism.

2000 In *Bush v. Gore*, the U.S. Supreme Court notes that the varying methods of recounting disputed votes in the state of Florida violates the equal protection clause of the Fourteenth Amendment, thus awarding Florida's electoral votes, and the presidency, to George W. Bush (2001–2009).

2006 The Voting Rights Act is extended for 25 years.

2009 Barack Obama, the nation's first African American president, is inaugurated as the 44th president of the United States; Obama nominates Sonia Sotomayor, who is confirmed, as the first Hispanic American associate justice of the U.S. Supreme Court.

Preface

The United States was founded on ideas. Those who wrote the U.S. Constitution were influenced by ideas that began in Europe: reason over religion, human rights over the rights of kings, and self-governance over tyranny. Ideas, and the arguments over them, have continued to shape the nation. Of all the ideas that influenced the nation's founding and its growth, 10 are perhaps the most important and are singled out here in an original series—KEY CONCEPTS IN AMERICAN HISTORY. The volumes bring these concepts to life, *Abolitionism, Colonialism, Expansionism, Federalism, Industrialism, Internationalism, Isolationism, Nationalism, Progressivism*, and *Terrorism*.

These books examine the big ideas, major events, and influential individuals that have helped define American history. Each book features three sections. The first is an overview of the concept, its historical context, the debates over the concept, and how it changed the history and growth of the United States. The second is an encyclopedic, A-to-Z treatment of the people, events, issues, and organizations that help to define the "-ism" under review. Here, readers will find detailed facts and vivid histories, along with referrals to other books for more details about the topic.

Interspersed throughout the entries are many high-interest features: "History Speaks" provides excerpts of documents, speeches, and letters from some of the most influential figures in American history. "History Makers" provides brief biographies of key people who dramatically influenced the country. "Then and Now" helps readers connect issues of the nation's past with present-day concerns.

In the third part of each volume, "Viewpoints," readers will find longer primary documents illustrating ideas that reflect a certain point of view of the time. Also included are important government documents and key Supreme Court decisions.

The KEY CONCEPTS series also features "Milestones in. . . ," time lines that will enable readers to quickly sort out how one event led to another, a glossary, and a bibliography for further reading.

People make decisions that determine history, and Americans have generated and refined the ideas that have determined U.S. history. With an understanding of the most important concepts that have shaped our past, readers can gain a better idea of what has shaped our present.

Jennifer L. Weber, Ph.D.
Assistant Professor of History, University of Kansas
General Editor

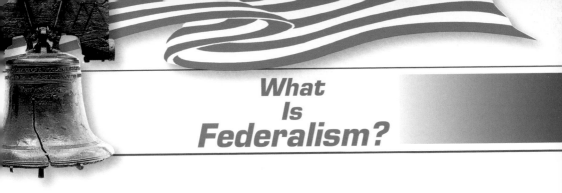

What Is Federalism?

Federalism is one kind of government. In a **federal** system, such as the American system, power is shared between a central government and regional governments.

Modern federalism first developed in the United States. Its concepts have proven to be widely acceptable to the vast majority of the American people. Today, the federal system of government is also used by many other countries around the world, including Canada, Mexico, and Brazil.

In 1787, American colonial leaders called for a convention to strengthen the Articles of Confederation. Rather than improve the Articles, however, the delegates created a new, federal system of government under the U.S. Constitution.

BASIC CONCEPTS: DIVISION OF POWERS

The first basic concept of American federalism is the division of governmental powers between a central government—the nation—and regional governments—the states. Based upon a written document, the Constitution, political power is divided between these two levels of government. Neither the central nor the regional level of government gets its power from the other.

The concept of a division of powers in the American government is based on several ideas. One is that the national government has certain specific powers that should be used to solve national problems. Within this area, the national government is supreme and cannot be contradicted by the states. These powers are limited by certain provisions in the Constitution and by constitutional changes that have come about through **amendment**, interpretation, custom, and usage.

A key idea underlying the concept of division of powers is the belief that, in general, all powers not delegated to the central government nor denied the states are powers that are reserved to the states. Under the Constitution, certain powers are specifically denied the states, or the right of the states to use them is restricted. Interpretations of the Constitution have tended to reduce some of the powers of the states and to expand the powers of the national government. As a result, the national government has become increasingly powerful, or dominant.

State Powers Despite increasing power within the central government, the principle of reserved powers for the states remains an essential part of the nation's federal system. The states retain and exercise substantial powers. These powers generally cover the fields of state and local law and law enforcement, taxation, education, elections, and voting qualifications. As long as state actions in these areas do not violate the Constitution, there is virtually no interference by the national government.

A Stable Union The concept of division of powers between regional units and the national government produced the unique type of federalism found in the United States. Through federalism, Americans were able to create a stable union among different units of government and still maintain a high degree of freedom, independence, and responsibility for each unit. In the past, confederations, such as the ancient Greek city-states, had lacked unity and stability.

BASIC CONCEPTS: UNITY AND DIVERSITY

A second key concept of modern American federalism is the belief in a system that offers both a degree of unity and, at the same time, allows a high degree of diversity from one area to the next. In this respect, a modern federal system often appears desirable for large nations with populations that have different backgrounds and different ways of life.

In the American federal system, specific issues that arise concerning education, for example, are usually handled at the state and local levels. Each state is responsible for its own educational system. Within each state, local communities select boards of education to direct the affairs of their schools according to state laws and regulations. Thus, each state can establish a system of education that is responsive to the wishes and requirements of its people, subject, of course, to the constitutional guarantees of equality of citizenship. Therefore, each community can adapt its school system to local needs and ways of life.

Development of New Ideas By allowing state governments to exercise their powers independently, federalism encourages the development of new ideas and methods to solve local problems. Over the years, many of these new approaches to local issues have proven so successful that they were adopted by other states or by the national government. Minimum-wage laws, unemployment compensation, and primary elections are all outgrowths of ideas first tried at the state or local levels.

REASONS FOR AMERICAN FEDERALISM

The Framers of the Constitution faced a number of serious problems in 1787. The central government created by the Articles of Confederation (1781–1789) did not have enough power to unify and strengthen the young nation. The problem was not easy to solve because, by 1787, most American people had become strongly attached to the idea of independent state governments. Indeed, people of the time referred to themselves as Virginians or New Yorkers first, and as Americans second. Thus, almost any attempt to establish a strong central government was bound to face opposition.

State Loyalties Most Americans of the post-Revolutionary period were strongly loyal to their states, perhaps because of their earlier colonial experience. Most American colonies had developed independently and had little contact with one another in the colonial period. They had been founded at different times and for different reasons. The differences among the colonies, coupled with the lack of any rapid means of communication, led to independent and somewhat different political, economic, and social developments in each of the colonies.

Thus, the people of the individual states failed to grow together as a politically unified nation immediately after the Revolutionary War (1775–1783). They had grown accustomed to solving their problems through local and state government agencies, rather than through a central authority.

To create a strong, unified nation, the Framers of the Constitution had to establish a political system that was acceptable to two opposing groups of people. The delegates had to design a political system that would appeal to those who wanted independent states with power to handle local affairs. At the same time, the delegates had to devise a system capable of handling national issues as well. The practical answer to this difficulty was a governmental system that offered both national stability and a meaningful role for the states. The solution was federalism.

Fear of Centralization A fear of centralized authority also arose out of the nation's colonial experience. This fear was a direct outgrowth of the restrictive colonial policies that the early colonists had experienced under the rule of **Great Britain**.

A number of years after the American Revolution, Thomas Jefferson warned, "If ever this vast country is brought under a single government, it will be one of the most extensive corruption." This statement was typical of the attitude of many Americans. The central authority of Great Britain had, during colonial times, imposed what many believed were oppressive and tyrannical regulations upon the people.

After this harsh experience, many Americans believed that the only way to prevent oppression and maintain their freedom was to keep government limited in power and close to the people, who could then control it. A strong central government, some people felt, might be beyond their immediate control and therefore could become oppressive.

In Article II of the Articles of Confederation, the document that in 1781 established only a loose alliance among the states, the emphasis was on a weak central authority and on free, independent states. This article stated:

> Each state retains its sovereignty, freedom and independence, and every Power, Jurisdiction and right, which is not by this confederation expressly delegated to the United States, in Congress assembled.

Soon, however, the distribution of power allowed under the Articles of Confederation proved to be ineffective. The logical solution to the problem was a federal system, where power and responsibility would be shared. Such a system could provide for a strong, but limited, central government as well as for a division of power between that government and the states.

THE FEDERAL EXPERIENCE: NULLIFICATION

A serious problem arose after the establishment of the nation's federal system of government. This issue was states' rights. Could states, it was asked, refuse to obey federal laws and withdraw from the Union? This question was raised when those who favored strong and independent states attempted to break the power of the federal government, first through **nullification** and later through secession, withdrawing from the Union.

The term *nullification* can be defined as a declaration by a state that a law passed by the national government is null and void and not binding on that state's citizens. The history of this idea is long and varied, and even today some people advocate this view. The first attempt to nullify a national law occurred in the late eighteenth century as a result of the Alien and Sedition Acts of 1798.

In 1798, the Federalist Party controlled the national government. The Jeffersonian Republicans strongly opposed the Federalists because of the Federalist's pro-British and anti-French foreign policies. To bring an end to the criticism of their policies, the Federalists succeeded in passing the Alien and Sedition Acts. Among other things, the law made it a crime to obstruct the policies of the national government or "defame" its officials. The act obviously struck at two basic freedoms—freedom of speech and freedom of the press. Under the leadership of Thomas Jefferson and James Madison, Virginia and Kentucky passed **resolutions** that rendered the act null and void. Other states, however, refused to follow suit, and the idea of nullification declined, particularly after the Federalists were defeated at the polls in the presidential election of 1800, which Thomas Jefferson won.

THE FEDERAL EXPERIENCE: SECESSION

The idea of nullification arose again, however, as did a related idea, secession—the withdrawal of a state from the Union. During the War of 1812 (1812–1814), opponents of the war discussed and proposed both nullification and secession. The end of the war in 1814 cut these discussions short, but in less than 15 years, the idea of nullification again gained support.

The renewal of support was largely the result of the efforts of John C. Calhoun of South Carolina. Once a supporter of national legislation, both as a member of Congress and vice president, Calhoun had by the late 1820s come to believe that some national policies, particularly protective **tariffs,** were contrary to the interests of his native state of South Carolina.

Calhoun's belief in nullification was based on two ideas. One, the states, not the people, had established the Constitution. Thus, if the national government had any power, it was power granted to it by the states, which could remove or restrict this power if they desired. Two, Calhoun believed that the states were **sovereign** and independent and therefore each state could judge national laws, declaring them null and void if they were contrary to the interests of the state.

On the basis of this doctrine, South Carolina declared the tariff acts of 1828 and 1832 null and void. The threat of a civil war over this issue was finally averted when Congress passed a compromise tariff in 1833. However, the ideas of nullification and secession still had supporters. Ultimately, the question of which was supreme—the states or the national government—was settled by the Civil War (1861–1865) and the defeat of the secessionist states in 1865.

Today, the idea of the supremacy, or dominance, of the national government is taken for granted. This is not, however, only the result of the victory of Union forces in the Civil War. Other events occurred that, as much as the Civil War, led to the general acceptance of a supreme national government within America's federalist system.

NATIONAL SUPREMACY

The belief in national supremacy was generally accepted by the nation's Founders. Even those delegates who supported a plan that gave broad powers to the individual states realized that treaties and national laws had to be the supreme law of the land.

During the first quarter of the nineteenth century, the U.S. Supreme Court became a major force in the conflict over national supremacy. Under the leadership of Chief Justice John Marshall, the Supreme Court interpreted the Constitution in ways that enlarged the powers of the national government and strengthened the concept of national supremacy. One example of this extension of national power is the Court's decision in *McCulloch v. Maryland* (1819).

A Decisive Case The case of *McCulloch v. Maryland* grew out of Maryland's attempt to hinder the operation of the national bank, which had been established by Congress. In effect, the state of Maryland was attempting to nullify a national law by obstructing the operation of the bank.

The Supreme Court's ruling against Maryland tax law had two results. First, it enlarged the power of the national government. It did this by upholding the right of Congress to establish a bank as part of its **implied powers**. Second, the decision prohibited the states from interfering with the exercise of Congress's powers—in this instance the power to operate a national bank without interference from state governments.

The Supreme Court's ruling in this and other cases was an essential step toward the public's acceptance of national supremacy within the federal system. Today, the vast majority of Americans accept the federal government as supreme. They view the states as individual semi-independent regional units that cooperate with the federal government to solve most problems and issues facing society. Yet, there is still a fear of "big government" that is shared by many Americans as well as the belief that the federal government should not abuse its power. As a result, there remains a strong belief among some Americans that the national government should not further increase its power.

FEDERALISM TODAY

The federal system of today is unlike that of 1900, and the system of 1900 was different from that before the Civil War. The nation's history shows a continual change in the relationship between the national government and the states. From year to year, the changes are small and may be barely noticeable, but over longer periods of time, they become apparent.

The United States of America

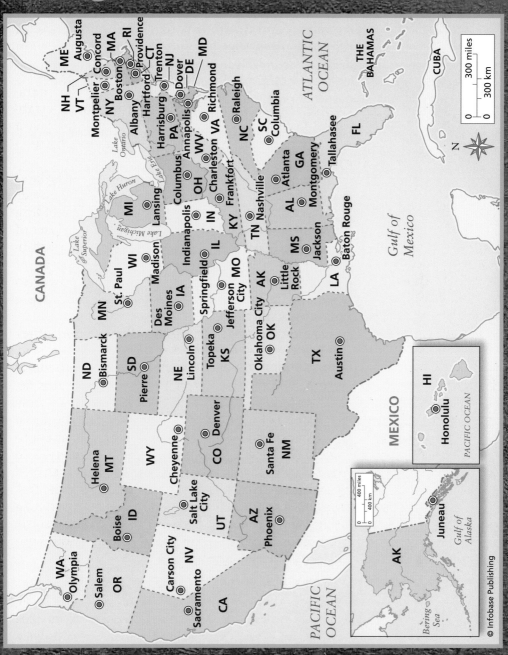

All of the nation's 50 states—from Rhode Island, the smallest state, to Alaska, the largest state—have equal rights under the nation's federal system of government. Political leaders have often disagreed about how much power the federal government should exercise over the states—an issue that remains today.

Today, the American federal system is a political system that has more than one center of power, energy, and creativity. It is a system characterized by a supreme central authority that shares powers with regional units that act independently in certain areas. It is a system of cooperating governmental units working together to solve local, regional, or national problems.

Both in theory and practice, American federalism has definite advantages as a method of governing the nation. It provides not only a system of limited government but also a system that can offer both unity and diversity. Another advantage is that the American federal system has made it possible for state and local governments to serve as training grounds for future national officials. State and local public offices provide hands-on political, legislative, and administrative experience for leaders who later become members of Congress or presidents.

FURTHER READING

Berkin, Carol. *A Brilliant Solution: Inventing the American Constitution.* New York: Harvest Books, 2003.

Collier, Christopher. *Decision in Philadelphia: The Constitutional Convention of 1787.* New York: Ballantine Books, 2007.

Genovese, Michael A., and Lori Cox Han. *Encyclopedia of American Government and Civics.* New York: Facts On File, 2008.

Madison, James, Edward J. Larson, and Michael P. Winship. *The Constitutional Convention: A Narrative from the Notes of James Madison.* New York: Modern Library, 2005.

A–B

Adams, John (1735–1826)

First vice president and second president (1797–1801) of the United States. John Adams was one of the nation's most important Founders, a leader whose political philosophies helped create the country's **federal** government and its system of **checks and balances** in the Constitution.

EARLY LIFE

Adams was born on October 30, 1735, in what was then Braintree, in the Massachusetts Bay Colony, to John and Susanna Adams. Despite believing that he would grow up to be a farmer, Adams proved to be a bright student. In addition to his local schooling, Adams studied Latin with a local tutor and passed the entrance exam to Harvard College in 1751.

Adams's time at Harvard intensified his interest in academic studies, and he gained renown as a philosopher, scientist, and speaker. He graduated in 1755 and, after a brief and unhappy stint as a schoolteacher in Worcester, Massachusetts, chose to pursue a career as a lawyer.

Adams's family was well connected, and he was introduced to lawyers in Boston. The men of Boston talked often about politics, especially after **Great Britain**'s Parliament passed the Stamp Act of 1765. Adams wrote a protest to this act, which brought him great acclaim throughout Massachusetts. He had also made a name for himself as a lawyer, and in 1770, the British soldiers involved in the **Boston Massacre,** a riot that ended with the deaths of five civilians, asked Adams to be their defense attorney. Despite being a **Patriot,** Adams argued for their defense and won, a testament to his professionalism.

By the time of the **Boston Tea Party** in 1773, Adams had become well known to the revolutionaries in Massachusetts. He wrote for their newspapers, and they came to him often for political advice in dealing with the governor of the **colony**, a man loyal to Britain. In 1774, Adams was elected Massachusetts' representative to the First Continental Congress in Philadelphia.

CONTINENTAL CONGRESSES

Adams's actions at the First Continental Congress (1774) and the Second Continental Congress (1775–1781) were among his most influential. His abilities as a philosopher and speaker fired up his fellow representatives. He pressed the cause of liberty, insisting that the American colonies should break away from Great Britain.

PUSH FOR INDEPENDENCE

In 1775, Adams continued to argue for independence during the meetings of the Second Continental Congress. Tensions with Great Britain were high. Shots had already been fired between disgruntled Patriots and British troops. Adams nominated George Washington (1732–1799) as the commander in chief of the American army, and the Congress voted to appoint him.

In 1776, Adams finally brought the issue of independence to a head. He put a proposal before the Continental Congress that the colonies should draft their own constitutions. This, too, was adopted. In addition, a committee was formed to write the Declaration of Independence. This committee included John Adams, Thomas Jefferson, Benjamin Franklin, Roger Sherman, and Roger R. Livingston. While Jefferson wrote the Declaration, it was Adams who argued for it on the floor of Congress. Jefferson called him their "Colossus," a man who supported the document with such force and passion that the delegates were moved.

After the passage of the Declaration on July 4, 1776, Adams's time was almost completely taken up by Congress, where he worked on 90 different committees. In 1778, he was made ambassador to France. This was an important position, as the young nation needed a military alliance with France. However, other delegates to France arranged the alliance before Adams arrived, so he returned to

Massachusetts. Adams later went to the Netherlands to work on the peace treaty that affirmed the United States' victory in the American Revolution (1775–1783). He then became the ambassador to Great Britain. From 1785 to 1787, he wrote *A Defence of the Constitutions of Government of the United States*, in which he argued for a bicameral government and a system of checks and balances. His positions were incorporated into the Constitution, which strengthened the federal government.

NATIONAL OFFICE

Although Adams went on to become George Washington's vice president and eventually president of the United States himself, his greatest influence was during these formative years of the Union, in which his passion for independence became a driving force for the nation. Throughout his long career, Adams remained committed to **federalist** principles.

See also: Jefferson, Thomas; Washington, George.

FURTHER READING

McCullough, David. *John Adams*. New York: Simon & Schuster, 2008.

Behrman, Carol H. *John Adams*. Minneapolis, Minn.: Lerner Books, 2003.

Thompson, C. Bradley. *John Adams & the Spirit of Liberty*. Lawrence: University Press of Kansas, 2002.

Albany Plan of Union (1754)

Proposal drafted by American diplomat and inventor Benjamin Franklin and designed to place **Great Britain**'s American **colonies** under a more centralized government. Franklin's Albany Plan of Union was a first move toward a **federalist** system of government for the thirteen colonies.

In 1754, representatives from Connecticut, New York, Maryland, Massachusetts, New Hampshire, Pennsylvania, and Rhode Island met in Albany, New York, at a meeting that became known as the Albany Congress. There, the representatives discussed several issues that concerned the colonies, namely, relations with Indian tribes and the defense of the colonies against the French. At the time, war was looming between Great Britain and France.

THE PLAN

The plan called for a loose union among 11 of the 13 colonies (Delaware and Georgia were omitted). Representatives, based on a colony's size and elected every three years, were to be sent to a Grand Council in Philadelphia. This **colonial government** was to be headed by a president-general who was appointed by the British Crown.

The Grand Council was given very specific legislative powers. Among these were the power to negotiate, in the name of the Crown, with the various Indian tribes and to make laws concerning trade with the Indians. In addition, the

Grand Council was given the authority to raise an army for the defense of the colonies and to levy and collect taxes to pay the soldiers. No laws passed by the Grand Council could contradict English law, however, and all colonial laws could be overturned by the British Crown. Finally, the Albany Plan of Union noted that the Grand Council did not replace either the colonial governments or the colonial militias.

A–B

Author, publisher, scientist, inventor, and statesman, Franklin was an early supporter of a federal system of government.

HISTORY MAKERS

Benjamin Franklin (1706–1790)

American **patriot,** diplomat, author, scientist, and inventor, Benjamin Franklin was born in 1706 in Boston, Massachusetts. At age 12, he was apprenticed to his older brother, James, a printer. The two brothers quarreled, and Benjamin ran away to Philadelphia, where he eventually set up his own print shop and published a widely read newspaper, *The Pennsylvania Gazette.*

In the 1730s, Franklin, along with other civic-minded Philadelphians, established the first library, which not only loaned books but also collected money with which to buy more books. In 1736, Franklin created the Union Fire Company in Philadelphia, the first volunteer fire department in the thirteen colonies.

The Pennsylvania Assembly sent Franklin as a representative to the Albany Congress, held in Albany, New York, in 1754. There, he proposed a plan for the colonies, known as the Albany Plan of Union. Although the plan was never implemented, it laid the foundation for uniting the colonies.

In 1776, Franklin was chosen by the delegates to the Second Continental Congress to be a member of the Committee of Five, who were charged with writing the **Declaration of Independence.** Later that year, in December, the Congress sent Franklin as the colonial representative to France. He succeeded in negotiating an alliance in 1778. Later, in 1783, Franklin served on the American delegation that hammered out and signed the Treaty of Paris, in which Britain recognized America's independence. His work in France complete, Franklin returned to the United States in 1785.

In 1787, the state of Pennsylvania sent Franklin to the Constitutional Convention in Philadelphia. Franklin is the only **Founder** to have signed the Declaration of Independence, the Treaty of Paris, and the U.S. Constitution.

The Albany Plan of Union was not intended as a plan for the colonies to become more independent from Britain. Instead, Franklin and the plan's other colonial supporters saw it as a way to improve relations with Britain.

SUPPORT AND OPPOSITION

Despite some support from both sides of the Atlantic, the Albany Plan never went into effect. The various colonial governments, realizing that the plan would diminish their own power, rejected the plan or failed to vote on it. Facing the possibility of war with France, the British took measures to ensure military order, as well as peace and trade with the Indians. The British sent General Edward Braddock to command British military forces throughout the colonies, and the Crown sent two commissioners to deal with the Indian tribes.

Although the Albany Plan failed, it was the first time that the individual colonies had worked so closely together. In fact, the plan served as a model for future plans of union; it was later used as the basis for the Articles of Confederation. The Albany Plan is noteworthy because it attempted to separate executive power, or the carrying out of the laws, from the legislative power, or the law-making function of government. This governmental trait, or **separation of powers,** is taken for granted today.

Furthermore, the plan envisioned the mainland American colonies as one unit, separate from British colonies in the West Indies and elsewhere. Although the Albany Plan was never executed, the ideas about an independent land were carried forward into the future.

See also: Articles of Confederation; Federalist System.

FURTHER READING

Fleming, Thomas. *Ben Franklin: Inventing America*. New York: Sterling Press, 2007.

Shannon, Timothy J. *Indians and Colonists at the Crossroads of Empire: The Albany Congress of 1754.* Ithaca, N.Y.: Cornell University Press, 2002.

Articles of Confederation (1781)

Document ratified on March 1, 1781, by the Continental Congress, to establish a central government for the United States. After the thirteen colonies declared independence from **Great Britain**, the newly established American republic needed a way to regulate the powers not contained within individual state constitutions.

Colonial leaders were wary of a strong central government, and for good reason. Colonial leaders believed that the English **monarchy** from which they had **seceded** abused power in order to levy taxes and restrict trade between the colonies and other non-British settlements. "The Articles of Confederation and Perpetual Union" was penned by John Dickinson, chair of the drafting committee, and presented to Congress on July 12, 1776.

BASIC POWERS

The Articles of Confederation reflected the **Founders'** aversion to large government and appealed to the states' desire for independence from powerful centralized rule. It established guidelines for state representation in the **federal** government, voting regulations, and control over newly acquired lands, while leaving all other regulation and taxation in the hands of the states, including the minting of money and assembling of an army.

The Articles of Confederation went through several rewrites before being ratified by all 13 states in 1781. They created the Congress of the Confederation, which became America's central ruling body. According to Article 3, the states were now united under a loose framework and labeled as:

a firm league of friendship with each other, for their common defense, the security of their liberties, and their mutual and general welfare, binding themselves to assist each other, against all force offered to, or attacks made upon them, or any of them, on account of religion, sovereignty, trade, or any other pretense whatever.

The leaders of each state recognized the benefits of uniting in defense and commerce, but they were reluctant to relinquish their autonomy. However, they embraced the ideals set forth by **Enlightenment** philosophers regarding republicanism, the idea that citizens of a nation can participate in government directly through the political process and indirectly through civic virtue—the good works of the community—while still remaining cautious of government corruption.

PROBLEMS WITH THE ARTICLES

Conflicts arose when the weakness of a small central government revealed flaws in the Articles of Confederation. Under the Articles, the central government was unable to levy taxes and therefore unable to establish financial order. Without the power to control commerce or mint money, the central government was unable to moderate competition between the states or establish a uniform method of currency exchange. Commerce relied on a mixture of coin and paper money issued by many states, all of which was rapidly losing value.

Before and during the American Revolution (1775–1783), many merchants relied on revenue generated by trade with Great Britain and its allies; that revenue vanished after America achieved its independence. Farmers suffered some of the greatest losses as food supply exceeded demand and their debts rose considerably. Many were forced to declare **bankruptcy.** A Massachusetts farmers' uprising, known as Shays's Rebellion, represented the desperation that existed among farmers before new trade laws were put into place.

Because most of the power rested in the hands of the states and because amendments to the Articles required a unanimous vote by all of the 13 entities, change was difficult to achieve. This requirement slowed down the effectiveness of the government for a country as large and diverse as the United States. Most of the states used a three-branch system of government—legislative, executive, and judicial. The central government, however, was set up with a **unicameral,** or single-branch, structure. There was no executive or judicial branch with which the legislature shared power. As a result, there were no **checks and balances** on the power of the government.

REPLACING THE ARTICLES

As the forerunner to the U.S. Constitution, the Articles of Confederation made great steps toward creating a successful federal government by outlining methods of governance that did not work for the new nation. The Founders learned that without uniform methods of governing across state lines, the central government would be unable to maintain social, military, and economic order, resulting in chaos for all citizens.

By issuing currency, the government would be able to maintain a uniform payment and credit system within its borders and facilitate specialization and trade across state lines. Many of the states had maintained their own armies, and some even had kept their own navies.

The U.S. Constitution was written to strengthen the weaknesses of the Articles of Confederation and establish a more powerful central government as part of a balanced federal nation, a nation in which the states and national governments share the responsibilities. Unlike the Articles of Confederation, the Constitution was designed to adapt to change, and it has successfully done so for more than 200 years.

See also: Constitutional Convention; Hamilton, Alexander; Shays's Rebellion; States' Rights; Washington, George.

FURTHER READING

Dougherty, Keith L. *Collective Action Under the Articles of Confederation.* West Nyack, N.Y.: Cambridge University Press, 2006.

Feinberg, Barbara. *The Articles of Confederation.* Minneapolis, Minn.: Twenty-first Century Books, 2002.

Rebman, Renee C. *The Articles of Confederation.* Minneapolis, Minn.: Compass Point, 2006.

Block Grants

Large **federal** awards of money to state and local governments; the funds give those governments great flexibility to design and implement a wide range of social programs appropriate for their needs. Federal requirements on how to spend block grants are minimal, giving the states more authority to determine how the money should be spent. Block grants have been an important tool of the American federal system since 1966.

HISTORY OF BLOCK GRANTS

President Lyndon B. Johnson (1963–1969), a Democrat, oversaw the enactment of the first two block grants—the Partnership for Health program (1966) and the Safe Streets program (1968). These two programs accounted for less than one percent of all federal aid to state and local governments.

Later, Republican presidents expanded the use of block grants. In 1971, President Richard M. Nixon (1969–1974) proposed consolidating 129 different programs into 6 block grants. A Democratic Congress rejected Nixon's original consolidation proposal. Nonetheless, by about 1976, Congress had created three new block grants. Two of these—the Community Development Block Grant (CDBG) and the Social Services Block Grant (SSBG)—are still in operation. Funding for the third, the Comprehensive Employment and Training Act (CETA) program, ended in 1982. It was replaced, however, by other job-training block grants.

The block grants of the 1970s provided more money than the programs they replaced. Thus, even states and cities that received an overall smaller share of federal aid still received more money than in the past.

In 1981, President Ronald Reagan (1981–1989) proposed consolidating 85 existing grants into 7 block grants. Instead, Congress combined 77 individual grants into 9 block grants. With the new programs, block grants now made up nearly 17 percent of federal aid. Unlike the Nixon block grants, however, the Reagan block grants provided about 25 percent less funding than the programs they replaced.

RECENT BLOCK GRANTS

A significant extension of block grants occurred in 1996. In that year, the Republican-controlled 104th Congress approved President Bill Clinton's (1993–2001) proposed Personal Responsibility and Work Opportunity Reconciliation Act. This welfare reform act replaced Aid to Families with Dependent Children (AFDC). At the same time, Congress also increased block grant funding for child care and some social services.

Block grants remain controversial. People who support block grants typically argue that programs will be more effective and better suited to each state because the decision making shifts to the states. Individuals who oppose block grants believe that state flexibility will be misused. They also argue that block grants reduce funding for key social programs.

See also: Federalist System; New Federalism; Nixon, Richard M.; Reagan, Ronald.

FURTHER READING

Gerston, Larry N. *American Federalism: A Concise Introduction.* New York: M.E. Sharpe, 2007.

Hickok, Eugene W. *Why States? The Challenge of Federalism.* Westminster, Md.: Heritage Books, 2007.

C

Calhoun, John C. (1782–1850)

Southern politician who served as a senator, congressman, secretary of war, secretary of state, and vice president. Calhoun fought for states' rights, rather than national authority, as a representative of his home state of South Carolina.

EARLY POLITICAL CAREER

In 1804, Calhoun graduated from Yale College (now Yale University) after just two years and then attended law school. In 1807, he became a lawyer in South Carolina. Calhoun's work as a lawyer quickly brought him into local and state politics. He was a member of the South Carolina state legislature from 1809 to 1811. In 1811, Calhoun was elected to the U.S. **House of Representatives**. Originally, he supported nationalist causes, such as a war with **Great Britain** in 1812 and the enlargement of the U.S. military. In 1817, Calhoun became President James Monroe's (1817–1825) secretary of war.

In the 1820s, however, Southern farmers were facing falling prices on their crops, and they blamed the **federal** government's **tariffs** on agricultural goods for their woes. This unrest back home led Calhoun to rethink his position on federalism.

NULLIFICATION AND SECESSION

In 1824, Calhoun was elected vice president under John Quincy Adams (1825–1829). He became vice president again in 1828 under Andrew Jackson (1829–1837). That same year, he secretly wrote the *South Carolina Exposition*, a letter to President Jackson detailing his state's objections to the Tariff of 1828, also called the "Tariff of Abominations." In the *Exposition*, Calhoun advocated his doctrine of **nullification,** or to declare a national law null and void within a state.

Since the writing of the Constitution in 1787, political leaders had discussed but never decided whether it was legal for a state to nullify a federal law. States' rights advocates, who placed the **sovereignty** of the state above that of the Union, believed that the individual states had the final say in which laws they would follow. Calhoun was among these, and he believed that South Carolina had the right to reject the tariff if it so chose, and further, to **secede** from the Union if it felt the need to do so.

When Congress and President Andrew Jackson refused to the repeal the tariff, South Carolina passed its own law, the Ordinance of Nullification, declaring the federal tariff void within the borders of South Carolina. This became known as the Nullification Crisis, and it was the final blow to Calhoun's and Jackson's already poor relationship. Calhoun resigned as Jackson's vice president in 1832 and reentered the **Senate**. Jackson threatened to "hang the nullifiers" and to use force, if necessary, to impose federal law. To avoid further crisis, Congress worked out a compromise tariff that lowered the tax rate over a period of years. Violence was temporarily avoided.

Following the Nullification Crisis, Calhoun became a proslavery advocate in Congress. He fought **abolitionists** on the Fugitive Slave Law and opposed the Wilmot Proviso (1846), which would have made slavery illegal in any land gained after the Mexican War (1846–1848). Calhoun argued that slavery was a positive good, as opposed to a necessary evil. He said that all societies are ruled by an upper class, which profits from the work of the lower classes. Instead of simply letting these lower classes struggle and die on their own, he said, enslaved people were taken care of by their owners, leaving them better off than the peasants in Europe or workers in the North. Calhoun's arguments came to define Southern **separatism**, and the division created by his fierce speechmaking helped move the country toward Civil War (1861–1865). Calhoun died on March 31, 1850.

See also: Jackson, Andrew; States' Rights; Virginia and Kentucky Resolutions.

FURTHER READING
Bartlett, Irving H. *John C. Calhoun: A Biography*. New York: W.W. Norton, 1994.

Census

A count of the national population, used to determine representation in the **House of Representatives**, the lower house of the U.S. Congress. The

Census is a key part of the nation's **federal** system of government because it determines each state's membership in the lower house of Congress.

CONSITUTIONAL MANDATE

Article I, Section 2, of the Constitution calls for a census to be conducted every 10 years of the "whole number of free persons." The delegates to the first Constitutional Convention decided that each state should have one representative for every 30,000 persons counted by the Census. This figure changed as the nation grew. Today, each member of the House represents about 650,000 people.

Counting the number of people in the United States has never been easy because of the political importance of the Census. The Census not only affects the reapportioning of House seats among the states, it also determines how district boundaries for state and local public officials are drawn and how billions of dollars in federal spending are distributed.

ISSUES

In 1911, Congress fixed the number of representatives at 435. Since then, a gain of representation in any one state can come only at the loss of representation in another. After the 1920 Census showed for the first time that the majority of Americans lived in cities, rural interests objected that the farm population had been undercounted.

The 1990 Census counted military personnel and their dependents stationed overseas. For the purposes of reapportionment, overseas personnel were assigned to the state that each individual considered home.

See also: Constitutional Convention; Federal Systems; Redistricting and Reapportionment.

Clay, Henry (1777–1852)

Known as the Great Compromiser and the Great Pacifier, a politician from Kentucky who served in both the U.S. **House of Representatives** and the **Senate**. He also sought the presidency three times. Clay struggled to find compromises that would save the nation's **federalist** system of government.

EARLY POLITICAL CAREER

In 1811, Clay was elected to the House of Representatives and became Speaker of the House that same year. As one of the War Hawks, a group of young politicians urging for war with Britain, he advocated for the War of 1812 (1812–1814) as a way for the United States to expand its borders. In particular, Clay hoped to add Canada to the nation. The United States failed to capture any Canadian territory, however, and the war ended in a stalemate.

THE MISSOURI COMPROMISE

Although he lived in a slave state, Henry Clay supported gradual **emancipation**. The issue of slavery became more pronounced during the early 1800s. After the American Revolution (1775–1783), most Northern states had passed laws that freed their slaves. At the same time, slavery became more profitable in the South, especially after 1793, when Eli

Whitney invented the cotton gin. This machine allowed the cotton seeds to be removed from the cotton fiber quickly and easily and performed the work of several slaves working by hand. The demand for cotton was increasing, especially in **Great Britain** as the industrial revolution took hold and textile mills opened, so Southern plantation owners expanded the number of acres of land devoted to cotton growing. In turn, this led to a demand for more slaves to work the fields.

By 1819, there were 22 states in the Union—11 that allowed slavery and 11 that did not. Thus, the balance of power in the U.S. Senate was equally divided between the free states and the slave states.

The Slavery Issue In 1818, Missouri petitioned to join the Union as a slave state. Northerners refused to allow Missouri's admission because it would upset the balance of power in the Senate and increase the power of the South. To solve this problem, Henry Clay suggested a plan that became known as the Missouri Compromise.

The Plan Under this plan, Missouri would be allowed to join the Union as a slave state, but in order to maintain balance, Maine—then a part of Massachusetts—would be admitted as a free state. In addition, slavery would be banned in all territories north of the 36'30° latitude line, except for Missouri. This would prevent future arguments, as the physical location of the new state would determine its status. Thus, Clay's compromise postponed a confrontation between the North and South, keeping the states united. The issue of slavery, however, would continue to plague the nation.

COMPROMISE OF 1850
The Mexican War (1846–1848) added half a million square miles of new territory to the United States, including the present-day states of California, Nevada, and Utah, and parts of Arizona, New Mexico, and Colorado. Then, in 1848, gold was discovered in California. Over the next year, thousands of gold-hungry miners descended on the area—enough people, in fact, to form a state. The California legislature petitioned Congress for permission to write a state constitution and seek admission to the Union. Arguments immediately began about whether California would be free or slave. Southerners were afraid that the admission of a free state would upset the balance of representation in Congress. Northerners feared that Texas, whose boundary with the New Mexico Territory was in dispute, would be divided into several new slave states.

Taylor's Recommendation President Zachary Taylor (1849–1850) advocated that both California and New Mexico should bypass the territorial stage and apply for statehood as free states. Once both had been admitted as states, residents in each could decide for themselves whether to remain free or allow slaves. Although Taylor was a Southerner and a slave owner, he was above all a president committed to maintaining the Union. Thus, when angry Southerners threatened to **secede,** he did what

President Andrew Jackson (1829–1837) had done decades earlier—he warned that he would use military force to maintain the Union if necessary.

Another Attempt at Compromise On January 29, 1850, Henry Clay, now 72 years old, gave a long speech to seek a compromise that would satisfy everyone and calm the nation. He introduced a bill that included five provisions: California would be admitted as a free state, and the rest of the territory acquired from Mexico would be organized into the territories of Utah and New Mexico without restriction on slavery. Texas's debt would be assumed by the **federal** government; the slave trade (but not slavery itself) would be abolished in the District of Columbia; and a stronger fugitive slave law would be created. However, opponents of certain sections combined to defeat Clay's bill. Clay's health was already declining, and the defeat sent him into retirement.

Illinois senator Stephen A. Douglas then took charge and pushed a series of five separate bills through Congress, rather than one large bill. Senators Daniel Webster of Massachusetts and John C. Calhoun of South Carolina gave heated speeches about the bills, while other politicians also argued their points of view. Suddenly, however, on July 9, 1850, President Taylor died after a brief illness, brought on by exposure to hot weather during Independence Day ceremonies in Washington.

The new president, Millard Fillmore (1850–1853), indicated that he was in favor of a compromise. He signed all five bills into law between September 9 and 20, 1850. Thus, once again, Henry Clay's compromise saved the Union.

See also: Jackson, Andrew; Calhoun, John C.; States' Rights; Webster, Daniel.

FURTHER READING
Remini, Robert V. *Henry Clay: Statesman for the Union.* New York: W.W. Norton & Company, 1993.

Connecticut Compromise

Also known as the Great Compromise, the plan adopted by delegates at the Constitutional Convention to solve the debate over how states should be represented in the national government. In 1787, the Constitutional Convention met in Independence Hall in Philadelphia, Pennsylvania, to draw up a document that would outline the structure and function of the new national government. One of the primary issues debated at the convention was how states would be represented in Congress, the new nation's lawmaking branch of government. Ultimately, the results of the Connecticut Compromise would form the basis of an essential part of the nation's **federal** system of government—providing for the structure of Congress.

THOUGHTS ON REPRESENTATION
During the convention, delegates from the large states argued for representation based on population. They believed that their comparatively larger financial contribution in

HISTORY MAKERS

Roger Sherman (1721–1793)

A signer of the Declaration of Independence and one of America's Founders, Roger Sherman is one of the lesser known figures to have influenced the formation of the United States. He was born in New Haven, Connecticut, on July 23, 1721.

He was elected to join the Continental Congress in 1774. Following the Revolutionary War (1775–1783), Sherman attended the Constitutional Convention of 1787 in Philadelphia to deal with the many problems facing the governance of the new nation.

A major point of conflict was the makeup of the **legislature.** The proposed Virginia Plan called for a bicameral legislature, with a lower house elected by the people. The members of the upper house would be elected by state legislatures, and each state would get representatives proportionally based on their population.

This proposal was unacceptable to smaller states, whose representatives felt that their concerns would always be overlooked by states with larger populations. Sherman and other small-state delegates then drafted the New Jersey Plan, in which the legislature would be a single house and each state would get one representative. Neither plan was popular enough to be passed, and the convention deadlocked.

Sherman then proposed a brilliant compromise. The lower house would determine the number of representatives based on the population of each state. In addition, the lower house would have exclusive rights to drafting bills on raising taxes and spending government funds. The smaller states would see their power in the upper house, in which every state would have two representatives, regardless of population. The compromise was adopted, and Sherman's design for the legislature became an essential part of the Constitution.

C

the form of tax revenue should earn them more votes in Congress. They sought to dismantle the "one state, one vote" tradition that had been in place during the American Revolution (1775–1783) and acquire a legislative advantage.

The Virginia Plan The Virginia Plan, drafted by James Madison and presented by the delegates from Virginia, reflected the wishes of the large states by proposing a **bicameral** legislature in which representation in both houses of the proposed Congress would be based on state population. Also known as the Large State Plan, it would allow representatives elected from the more populous states to pass legislation that would only benefit those states. Delegates from the small states stood in stark opposition and fought to protect their position against the power of the large states.

The New Jersey Plan In turn, William Paterson presented the New Jersey Plan, also known as the Small State Plan, to the convention on June 15, 1787. It preserved the "one state, one vote" system by calling for a single-chamber Congress based on equal representation for all states. Such a plan would have allowed representatives from the smaller states to vote with power equal to that of the large states, preventing the passage of bills that would favor any one region at the cost of another.

DEBATE AND AGREEMENT

The debate was fierce, and the deadlock threatened to prevent the convention from moving forward. Sherman and a small group of other delegates met privately to draw up a new plan that would appeal to both sides. The plan came to be known as the Connecticut Compromise and combined aspects of both the Virginia Plan and the New Jersey Plan. It called for a bicameral legislature consisting of one house in which the votes would be based on state population and another house in which each state would receive equal voting power. Though the plan was not immediately approved, proponents of the plan spoke on its behalf, and it was included as a key part of the U.S. Constitution in mid-July 1787.

The legislative branch would consist of an upper house, known as the **Senate**, and a lower house, referred to as the **House of Representatives**. Representation in the Senate would be equal, assigning two seats to each state for terms of six years. Representation in the lower house would be based on population.

A LONG-LASTING AGREEMENT

The Articles of Confederation (1781–1789) had created a weak central government with a **unicameral** legislature. The lack of a separation of powers and inability to control finances led Roger Sherman to draw up a solution that would replace the former unicameral legislature with the structure established by the Connecticut Compromise. Thus, the Connecticut Compromise created a balance of legislative power that has endured for more than 200 years.

See also: Articles of Confederation; Constitutional Convention.

FURTHER READING

Collier, Christopher. *Decision in Philadelphia: The Constitutional Convention of 1787.* New York: Ballantine Books, 2007.

Morton, Joseph C. *Shapers of the Great Debate at the Constitutional Convention of 1787: A Biographical Dictionary.* Westport, Conn.: Greenwood Press, 2005.

Constitutional Convention

Held in the summer of 1787, the assembly of delegates from 12 of the 13 states that created the present plan of government of the United States. The Constitutional Convention laid the foundation of our **federal** system of government, which has endured for more than 200 years.

The Constitutional Convention was held in Philadelphia, which was by far the largest American city at the time, with a population of around

45,000. Philadelphia's central location was a key reason the city was chosen as the convention site.

DELEGATES

The states selected delegates to represent their views at the convention. About 60 to 75 delegates were chosen in all; however, only 55 actually attended. The delegates were generally united in their belief that a stronger national government was needed. In part, this was because many of them had shared similar experiences. Forty-two were current or former members of Congress; 21 had fought in the Revolutionary War (1775–1783); and 8 had signed the Declaration of Independence (1776).

Other characteristics contributed to the delegates' common outlook as well. Almost all were prosperous—around half were lawyers and another quarter owned plantations or large farms. Only two delegates were small farmers, who made up 85 percent of the nation's white population. All had held public office. More than 40 occupied positions in their state governments, including 10 judges, 30 legislators, and 3 governors. Several had helped to write their state constitutions. All were well known in their states. About one-fourth had national reputations.

All of the delegates to the convention were white men. All but the two Roman Catholics were Protestant Christians. Twenty-six had attended college, at a time when a college education was rare.

THE VIRGINIA PLAN

The Virginia Plan, introduced on May 29 by Governor Edmund Randolph but written mainly by James Madison, offered a major change from the weak, **unicameral** government of the Articles of Confederation. The plan proposed the creation of a three-branch national government.

According to the Virginia Plan, the heart of the national government would be a **bicameral** legislature, with the lower house apportioned according to population and its members selected by the people, and the upper house elected by the lower house. The legislature's powers would include authority to pass laws, to conduct foreign policy, and to appoint most government officials, including judges. A national judiciary, organized into one or more "supreme tribunals" would form a second branch. The government also would have an executive branch, although it was vaguely defined in the Virginia Plan.

THE NEW JERSEY PLAN

One part of the Virginia Plan was especially controversial—the provision that both houses of the national legislature be apportioned according to population. Delegates from the large states—Virginia, Massachusetts, and Pennsylvania—and the three states whose populations were growing most rapidly—Georgia, North Carolina, and South Carolina—favored the idea. They split sharply with the delegates from the small states who feared that their citizens would be outnumbered in the legislature.

Thus, the small states favored the arrangement as laid out in the Articles of Confederation—equal representation in Congress for each state. The small states responded to the Virginia Plan with a counterproposal of their own that was introduced on June 15, 1787, by William Paterson of New Jersey.

Amending the Articles The New Jersey Plan was essentially a series of amendments to the Articles of Confederation. It proposed to add two new branches to the one-branch national government—a plural, or committee-style, executive, to be elected by Congress for a single term and a supreme court. The plan also would declare national laws and treaties to be "the supreme law of the respective States."

More Congressional Power Congress also would be empowered to regulate interstate and international

HISTORY MAKERS
James Madison (1751–1836)

One of the nation's Founders and the fourth president of the United States (1809–1817), James Madison was born in Port Conway, Virginia, in 1751. In 1769, he entered what is now Princeton University, then called the College of New Jersey. He completed a four-year degree in two years and graduated in 1771. This aptitude for learning contributed greatly to Madison's role as the "Father of the Constitution."

Before attending the Constitutional Convention as a representative from Virginia, Madison undertook a massive study of government. He wrote his findings into a document called "Notes on Ancient and Modern Confederacies."

Following this study of ancient confederacies, Madison made similar notes on the failures of the Articles of Confederation. Madison then narrowed down the problem of government to a single question: How could you create a system that would take advantage of people's natural tendency toward self-interest? In other words, how could you turn people's inherent self-interest into a system of government that would promote the greater good?

His studies made James Madison the most prepared of the delegates at the Constitutional Convention. Madison had concluded that a large country with a strong central government was the only option. By forming a large republic, people would have the opportunity to join many factions, each with their own interests. The number of such self-interested groups, however, would be so great that none of them could gain enough power to control the others. Thus, they would be forced to work together. Self-interest would breed cooperation.

Most of Madison's ideas for the Constitution were written into his Virginia Plan. Although many of the details were changed by Roger Sherman's Great Compromise, the overall shape of the Virginia Plan remained, and the United States is organized by these principles today.

commerce and to impose taxes. The main purpose of the New Jersey Plan, however, was an unstated one: to preserve the structure of Congress under the Articles—a single house in which each state, regardless of size, would cast one vote.

CONVENTION DEBATE

On June 20, 1787, with Virginian George Washington as president of the convention, the delegates began their clause-by-clause evaluation of the plans of government. The issue of legislative apportionment took most of the convention's time and attention during the five weeks of debate. Delegates from the small states pressed for equal representation of the states in Congress. The large-state delegates were equally unyielding in their insistence on representation according to population.

A special committee, with members from every state, was appointed on July 2 to seek a compromise. On July 5, after a break to celebrate Independence Day, the committee recommended a compromise plan proposed by Roger Sherman of Connecticut. The upper house would have equal representation from each state. The lower house would be apportioned according to population (with each slave counted as three-fifths of a person).

For more than a week, the delegates engaged in a sometimes bitter debate over the proposal. On July 16, the convention voted narrowly to approve the main points of the compromise proposal, sometimes called the Connecticut Compromise in honor of its author, Roger Sherman.

A COMMITTEE OF DETAIL

On July 24, 1787, the convention voted to appoint a Committee of Detail to review all of its actions and draft a plan of government. Most of the memorable terms and phrases in the Constitution were written by the Committee of Detail, including "state of the Union" and "We the People." Institutions were named: The executive became the "president"; the national tribunal, the "Supreme Court"; and the legislature, "Congress," with its upper house called the "**Senate**" and the lower house the "**House of Representatives**."

CONVENTION REVIEW

As they had with the Virginia Plan and the New Jersey Plan, the delegates reviewed the draft constitution that was proposed by the Committee of Detail clause by clause. Much of the draft was approved. Some parts, however, were modified, and the delegates tinkered with several provisions of the Committee of Detail's draft. For example, a procedure was created to amend the Constitution:

> . . . on the application of the legislatures of two-thirds of the states in the Union for an amendment of this Constitution, the legislature of the United States shall call a convention for that purpose.

In addition, religious tests were prohibited as a requirement for holding office. Finally, the delegates decided that the new constitution would take effect when 9 of the 13 states **ratified** it.

CONTROVERSIES

Some sections of the Committee of Detail's draft became matters of serious controversy. The draft constitution's stand on slavery was attacked by several Northern delegates. They opposed the three-fifths rule, which provided for counting three-fifths of the slaves as part of the population. They were also angered by the provision against laws banning the importation of new slaves. Southern delegates defended the provisions protecting slavery. They even insisted that their states would not ratify any constitution that placed slavery at risk.

As it had with the large state-small state disagreement, the convention appointed a special committee on August 22, 1787, to seek a compromise solution. Two days later, the committee proposed that Congress be authorized, if it so decided, to end the importation of slaves after 1800. In the meantime, Congress could tax imported slaves at a rate no higher than $10 each. The committee's recommendation passed.

Controversies over two other matters caused the convention to bog down—the powers of the Senate and issues regarding presidential selection. On August 31, nearing the end of its labors, the convention appointed a Committee on Postponed Matters, with a member from each state delegation, to resolve these difficult issues.

COMMITTEE ON POSTPONED MATTERS

Beginning on September 4, 1787, the Committee on Postponed Matters made several recommendations concerning the presidency. The committee proposed a term of four years rather than seven, with no restriction on the president's eligibility for re-election. The president was to be chosen by an **Electoral College.** To make up the Electoral College, each state would select, by whatever means it chose, electors equal in number to its representatives and senators in Congress. The candidate who received the greatest number of **electoral votes** would become president. The candidate who finished second would become vice president. (This was the first mention of the vice presidency at the convention.) If no candidate received a majority, the Senate would select a president and vice president from among the five candidates who had received the greatest number of electoral votes.

Details Concerning the President and Vice President In addition to its proposal for an Electoral College, the committee recommended that certain responsibilities be assigned to the vice president. The office's major duties would be to preside over the Senate, with the right to cast tie-breaking votes, and to act as president if that office became vacant before the expiration of the president's term.

Finally, the committee recommended that qualifications for president be stated in the Constitution. The president would have to be at least 35 years old, a natural-born citizen of the United States or a citizen at the time of the Constitution's enactment, and a resident of the United States for at least 14 years.

For several days, the delegates studied the committee's complex proposal for presidential selection. On September 7, they passed it after making only one substantial change: The House of Representatives, rather than the Senate, would choose the president in the event of an Electoral College deadlock, with each state delegation casting one vote. The Senate still would choose the vice president if the Electoral College failed to produce a winner.

Approval On September 8, the convention approved two final proposals of the Committee on Postponed Matters. The president was to be **impeached** by the House and, on grounds of "treason or bribery or other high crimes and misdemeanors against the United States," removed from office on conviction by the Senate. The delegates added the vice president and other civil officers to the roster of those subject to impeachment but raised the majority needed for Senate conviction from a simple majority to a two-thirds majority. In addition, the House was empowered to originate "all bills for raising revenue."

Having completed their work on the Constitution, the delegates ended the day's business on September 8, 1787, by voting to create a five-member Committee of Style. This committee was to write a polished, final draft for the delegates to sign. Among the committee's members were Gouverneur Morris (who seems to have done most of its work), James Madison, and Alexander Hamilton.

FINAL ADJUSTMENTS

Even as the Committee of Style labored, the convention continued to modify its earlier decisions. On September 10, 1787, Madison urged that special constitutional conventions not be a part of the process of amending the Constitution. Instead, he argued, amendments should be initiated by a two-thirds vote of Congress or by two-thirds of the state legislatures, with approval by three-fourths of the states needed for **ratification**. The Committee of Style incorporated Madison's idea into its draft.

On September 12, Hugh Williamson of North Carolina successfully moved that the requirement for overriding a president's **veto** be reduced from a three-fourths vote of each house of Congress to a two-thirds vote.

FINAL DRAFT

The committee's draft met with widespread approval from the delegates, but their tinkering continued. A provision was added that the Constitution could not be altered to deprive a state of equal representation in the Senate without the state's consent. At the initiative of Gouverneur Morris and Elbridge Gerry, a compromise procedure for amending the Constitution was created that incorporated both the Committee of Detail's recommendation and Madison's plan. As finally agreed, a constitutional amendment could be proposed by either a two-thirds vote of both houses of Congress or a convention that

C

Congress was required to call if two-thirds of the state legislatures requested one. In either case, three-fourths of the states would have to ratify an amendment for it to become part of the Constitution.

The convention's labors completed, the delegates assembled on September 17, 1787, to sign an **engrossed,** or final, copy of the Constitution. (This is the copy on public display at the National Archives in Washington, D.C.) Forty-one of the original 55 delegates still were present at the convention, and all but Edmund Randolph, George Mason, and Elbridge Gerry signed the document.

Later, as the last delegates waited to affix their signatures to the Constitution, Benjamin Franklin gestured to Washington's chair and said to those standing nearby:

I have often in the course of this session . . . looked at that sun behind the President without being able to tell whether it was rising or setting. But now, at length, I have the happiness to know that it is a rising and not a setting sun.

Even later that day, according to an oft-repeated story, someone asked Franklin as he left the hall,

"Well, Doctor, what have we got? A republic or a monarchy?" "A republic," Franklin replied, "if you can keep it."

See also: Connecticut Compromise; Federalist System; States' Rights; Washington, George.

FURTHER READING

Berkin, Carol. *A Brilliant Solution: Inventing the American Constitution.* New York: Harvest Books, 2003.

Collier, Christopher. *Decision in Philadelphia: The Constitutional Convention of 1787.* New York: Ballantine Books, 2007.

Madison, James, Edward J. Larson, and Michael P. Winship. *The Constitutional Convention: A Narrative from the Notes of James Madison.* New York: Modern Library, 2005.

Constitution of the United States

See Constitutional Convention.

D–F

Direct Popular Election and Federalism

The ability of voters to cast ballots directly for candidates within the nation's system of government, thus ensuring that the government reflects the will of the people. In the United States, most provisions for elections are established by state laws. The state, county, and city governments—not the **federal** government—arrange for elections and establish the conditions under which those elections are held.

SENATORIAL REPRESENTATION

The Framers of the U.S. Constitution believed, in theory, that the **Senate** represented the states, not the people. Thus, each state has two senators, regardless of size. Most of the Framers were uneasy about popular rule. The Constitution, therefore, provided for the election of senators by the state legislatures. This sort of indirect election was to be a check on hasty or unwise action by the people.

MOVE TO DEMOCRACY

By the late 1800s, however, many people became convinced that a popular vote was more democratic. Other people were certain that the indirect election of senators meant that they were selected by powerful and corrupt business interests. Because the Constitution specifically stated how senators were to be chosen, change in the election procedures would require a constitutional **amendment**.

Amending the Constitution, however, is not a simple task. Action can be initiated by a two-thirds majority vote of Congress or by a special convention called by Congress at the request of two-thirds of the state legislatures. In addition, any proposed amendments must be **ratified** by the state legislatures or by special conventions in three-fourths of the states.

Because few senators favored popular election—fearful that they might lose their seats—Congress did not act. However, the advocates of direct election were persistent. By 1910, they had convinced most state legislatures to select candidates nominated in direct **primary elections,** thus allowing the will of the voters to prevail. In 1912, Congress finally did approve an amendment calling for direct popular election of senators. After **ratification** by the required number of states legislatures in 1913, it became the Seventeenth Amendment to the Constitution.

Thus, with the direct popular election of senators, Congress, and the Senate in particular, came to better represent the will of the voters.

See also: Constitutional Convention; Seventeenth Amendment.

FURTHER READING

Genovese, Michael A., and Lori Cox Han. *Encyclopedia of American Government and Civics.* New York: Facts On File, 2008.

Elastic Clause

D–F

Article I, Clause 8, Section 18, of the U.S. Constitution. It provides the constitutional basis for the **implied powers** of Congress and is sometimes called "the necessary and proper clause." Through the use of the elastic clause, Congress has expanded its powers greatly during the nation's history.

VAST POWERS

Under its powers to regulate interstate **commerce**, for example, Congress has used its implied powers to legislate on a wide variety of subjects. Congress has determined that anything indirectly—in other words, not just directly—related to interstate commerce comes under this power. Thus, Congress legislates on the production as well as the distribution of goods and services involved in interstate commerce.

The implied powers of Congress cover a wide range of possibilities—and a key requirement of their use is simply that implied powers be exerted in conjunction with one of Congress's expressed powers. For example, from the expressed powers of

History Speaks

Article 1, Section 8, Clause 18

Article 1, Section 8, Clause 18, of the U.S. Constitution, also known as the elastic clause, gives Congress the flexibility to pass legislation that will keep pace with modern society. For example, although the Constitution says nothing about an air force, Article 1, Section 8, Clause 18, combined with the expressed power to maintain an army and a navy, implies that the United States can support an air force—something obviously beyond the dreams of the Founders in 1787. In addition, the Supreme Court, through landmark rulings such as *McCulloch v. Maryland* (1819) and *Gibbons v. Ogden* (1824), has affirmed this broad interpretation of this clause.

To make all Laws which shall be necessary and proper for carrying into Execution the foregoing Powers, and all other Powers vested by this Constitution in the Government of the United States, or in any Department or Officer thereof.

Congress to provide an army and a navy, it is *implied* that Congress also may maintain an air force. From the power of Congress to coin money, it is *implied* that Congress may also establish banks.

STRICT CONSTRUCTIONISTS

From the nation's beginning, the country's leaders have held differences of opinion about the doctrine of implied powers. A very strict, or narrow, interpretation of the doctrine was held by Thomas Jefferson (1801–1809), who insisted that "necessary and proper" meant that Congress had the power to do only those things that became absolutely essential to carry out its other powers. To support their view, Jefferson and his followers cited the Tenth Amendment:

The powers not delegated to the United States by the Constitution, nor prohibited by it to the states, are reserved to the states respectively, or to the people.

The advocates of Jefferson's view thus insisted that not everything that might seem proper was by any means *necessary*. They maintained that all kinds of proper actions might be better left to the states. Thus, Jefferson and his followers became known as *strict* constructionists.

LOOSE CONSTRUCTIONISTS

In contrast, Alexander Hamilton and his followers held the opposite view.

Hamilton argued for a broad interpretation of the necessary and proper clause. He maintained that this clause gave Congress the authority to do whatever was appropriate in carrying out its expressed powers. Hamilton and his followers became known as *loose* constructionists. Over time, the views of Hamilton and his followers have generally prevailed. Throughout the years, Congress has enacted huge amounts of legislation for which it was granted no specifically expressed powers.

See also: Hamilton, Alexander; Jefferson, Thomas; Loose Constructionist; States' Rights; Strict Constructionist; Tenth Amendment.

Electoral College System

Institution established by the Constitution to choose the president of the United States. Although the United States holds a popular election for president every four years, the winner is not actually determined by the outcome of the **popular vote.** Instead, **electors** from each state cast votes that are intended to reflect the will of the voters.

EARLY HISTORY
The Framers of the Constitution did not trust the common people and were unwilling to accept direct popular election of the president. They intended to leave selection of the president to the country's most learned and distinguished citizens in the states. These presidential electors made up the **Electoral College** and were chosen by the states. Because the states could determine

the method of selecting the electors, the Electoral College reinforced the **federal** system within the United States. Until 1832, there were three basic methods for choosing electors: popular vote in statewide contests, popular vote in district contests, and selection by state legislatures.

This changed with the growth of political parties, however. Political parties began to back statewide popular elections, which would allow the winning party to control all of the state's electors. By 1836, all states except South Carolina were choosing electors by statewide popular vote. South Carolina finally adopted popular voting for presidential electors after the Civil War (1861–1865). Since that time, a winner-takes-all popular vote for electors has been the almost universal practice, except for a few isolated cases.

In 1969, the Maine legislature enacted a district system for choosing presidential electors. Two of the state's four electors are selected by statewide vote, while the other two are awarded to the party that wins each of the state's two congressional districts. The system is still in force in Maine and has also been adopted by Nebraska.

HOW ELECTORS VOTE
When voters go to the polls on Election Day, they see the names of presidential candidates on the ballot. However, they are actually casting their votes for electors who have pledged to vote for the candidate who wins the state's popular vote. The electors usually are chosen at state party meetings called caucuses,

A Close Race

The election of 2000 was the closest presidential race in 40 years, and its result returned the Republican Party to the White House. The election brought the nation to the brink of a constitutional crisis within the nation's federal system, one that was narrowly averted only after an extraordinary 36 days of bitter arguing and lawsuits over who had won, Democrat Al Gore or Republican George W. Bush. The eventual outcome, with Texas governor Bush the official winner, did little to unite the electorate. The voters had split 100 million votes almost evenly between the two major-party candidates.

Although Gore, the **incumbent** vice president, won the national popular vote in the 2000 race by more than a half-million votes, Bush claimed the 25 electoral votes of Florida, where the election had been extremely close. Ultimately, the state's Republican administration, headed by Governor Jeb Bush (George W.'s brother), certified George W. Bush as the popular vote winner in Florida, raising the GOP candidate's nationwide **electoral vote** total to 271—just one more than Bush needed to win. Vice President Gore unsuccessfully contested the election on grounds that the state had stopped the recounts prematurely, leaving thousands of machine-processed ballots not subjected to a hand recount.

In the end, a sharply divided U.S. Supreme Court halted the Florida count, effectively deciding the election in Bush's favor. This modern race was the first time that the U.S. Supreme Court had taken up a lawsuit related to a presidential election. In the past, the Court had left such matters to Congress or to the states.

---

at party conventions, or in **primary elections**.

Disputed Electoral Votes The Constitution provides no guidelines for handling disputed electoral ballots. This has led several times to disagreement. The electoral bargain that settled the presidential election of 1876, for example, created one of the country's greatest electoral crises.

Early election night returns indicated that Democrat Samuel Tilden had been elected over Republican Rutherford B. Hayes. Tilden led the popular vote by more than a quarter-million votes. However, by the following morning it was clear that if the Republicans could win South Carolina, Florida, and Louisiana, Hayes would win 185 electoral votes to 184 for Tilden. If a single elector in any of those states voted for Tilden, it would throw the election to the Democrats. To complicate matters, several states filed two sets of electoral vote counts, and in Oregon, the legal eligibility of one Republican elector was in question.

To solve the dilemma, Congress established a 15-member Electoral Commission that had final authority over disputed electoral votes. In every disputed case, the commission voted 8–7 for Hayes, with all eight Republican members backing Hayes. Angry

Democrats in the House threatened to launch a **filibuster** so that the vote count could not be completed before inauguration day. Hayes's backers, however, reached a compromise with Southern Democrats. In return for their support, Hayes agreed to withdraw federal troops that had occupied the South since the end of the Civil War and to make other concessions. On March 2, 1877, Congress declared Hayes (1877–1881) the winner.

1887 Law Not until 1887 did Congress enact permanent legislation to handle disputed electoral votes. The Electoral Count Act of that year gave each state final authority in determining whether its choice of electors was legal. Challenged electoral votes could be sustained by Congress only upon majority vote of both the House and **Senate**. The act also established procedures to guide Congress in counting the electoral votes.

The election of 1876 also pointed out another controversial aspect of the Electoral College system—the fact that a candidate can win the popular vote yet lose the electoral vote. This has happened three other times in U.S. history: in 1824, 1888, and 2000.

The Election of 2000 The presidential election of 2000 between incumbent Vice President Al Gore and Texas governor George W. Bush (2001–2009) was the closest in 40 years. The election brought the nation to the brink of a constitutional crisis that was narrowly averted only after an unprecedented 36 days of bitter arguing and lawsuits.

Although Gore won the national popular vote in the 2000 race by more than a half-million votes, Bush claimed the 25 electoral votes of Florida, where the election had been extremely close. The close election triggered an automatic machine recount, which showed Bush ahead by only about 300 votes in Florida. Because of Florida's outdated voting machines and ballots that had been rejected by those machines, Gore's legal team challenged the state's decision.

Supreme Court ruling After several lawsuits at the state level, the U.S. Supreme Court halted the ongoing recounts pending its decision in *Bush v. Gore*. In its 5–4 decision, handed down on December 12, the Court majority ruled for Bush that the lack of uniform standards for manual recounts denied "equal protection of the laws" to Florida voters. That evening Bush was declared the Florida winner by 537 votes out of 6 million cast. Thus, Bush earned 271 electoral votes—just one more than the number needed to win the election—to Gore's 266. One elector from the District of Columbia abstained.

FAITHLESS ELECTORS
Nothing in the Constitution requires electors to vote in any particular way. Regardless of his or her party affiliation, an elector cannot be forced to vote for the party's candidate for president. In practice, almost all electors do vote for their party's candidate, but legally they are free to vote for whomever they choose. This so-called faithless-elector issue has been a long-standing controversy. On at

least nine occasions, presidential electors voted for a candidate other than their own party's choice. In none of these instances, however, did the switch alter the election result.

See also: Constitutional Convention; Political Parties; Reapportionment and Redistricting.

FURTHER READING

Hewson, Martha S. *The Electoral College.* New York: Chelsea House, 2002.

Morris-Lipsman, Arlene. *Presidential Races: The Battle for Power in the United States.* Minneapolis, Minn.: Twenty-first Century Books, 2007.

Federal City: Washington, D.C.

The nation's capital, which occupies a unique position within the **federal** system. The capital is neither a state nor a **territory.** The Framers of the Constitution decided that the capital of the new government should be located outside the control of any state.

EARLY HISTORY
In 1790, Congress approved a site selected by President George Washington (1789–1797) along the Potomac River. The site was named the District of Columbia after Christopher Columbus. It consisted of a 67-square-mile (174 km²) area carved from the state of Maryland and separated from Virginia by the Potomac River.

The area where the federal buildings were to be located was named the City of Washington. Pierre-Charles l'Enfant designed the city plan in 1791. L'Enfant was an army engineer who had come from France with General Lafayette to fight in the American Revolution (1775–1783).

Since that time, the city has grown and spread. Today, Washington, D.C., and the District of Columbia are one and the same. The site that was chosen more than 200 years ago as the nation's capital is now home to almost 600,000 people.

GOVERNING THE DISTRICT
Under the Constitution, Congress has final legislative authority over the District of Columbia. In its early history, the District enjoyed limited self-government and elected a mayor and a council. This arrangement ended in 1874. For the next 100 years, the District was governed by a board of three commissioners appointed by the president.

All the while, the citizens of the District continued to push for **home rule.** Finally, in 1973, Congress passed the Home Rule Act. The District approved the act, and in 1975, an elected mayor and council took office.

Under home rule, the District functions like a city and also like a state. The mayor is the chief executive of the District government, holding the powers of a city mayor and most of the powers of a state governor. The council is the city's legislative body. Its powers are similar to those of a state legislature.

Congress, however, safeguards the federal buildings and other interests in the nation's capital. Legislation enacted by the District council is sent to Congress for review. The law takes effect after 30 working days unless it is vetoed by both houses of Congress. In addition, under its constitutional

An engraving from the early 1800s shows the Capitol in the new federal city of Washington, D.C. Expanded and renovated over the years, the Capitol has remained a symbol of the nation's federal system of government. The states' 100 senators and 435 representatives meet in the Capitol to make laws for the nation.

authority, Congress can enact laws on any subject dealing with the District.

VOTING

The home-rule campaign was accompanied by a movement to give District residents the right to vote. The Twenty-third Amendment (1961) gave the District three electoral votes in presidential elections. However, its residents still had no representative in Congress. In 1970, Congress granted the District the authority to elect a nonvoting delegate to the **House of Representatives**.

In 1978, Congress proposed an amendment that would give voting representation in both the House and the **Senate** "as though it were a state." The proposal provided for the election of two senators and the number of representatives that the District's population would deserve if it were a state. However, the amendment was not **ratified** by the necessary three-fourths of the states. Thus, Washington, D.C., retains its unique position within the nation's federal system.

See also: Federalist System; Washington, George.

FURTHER READING

Bordewich, Fergus. *Washington: The Making of the American Capital.* New York: Amistad, 2008.

Franklin, Paul M. *Our Washington, D.C.* Osceola, Wis.: Voyageur Press, 2006.

Federalist System

A type of government in which power is shared between regional or state governments and a central, or **federal**, government. In a federal system, power and authority are shared according to the terms of a written agreement—a constitution.

ELEMENTS OF A FEDERAL SYSTEM

A written agreement is the first element of a federal system. It is needed to maintain a balance in the sharing of powers between the central government and the government's branches, and the nation's state and local governments. A constitution is essential.

The second element of every federal system is a number of major regional units, which, in the United States, are called *states*. In many other countries, such as Canada, these units are called *provinces*. Each of the political subdivisions of a nation has its own government and has final authority on some matters while sharing other powers with the central government.

A third element of a federal system is a central government with final authority on matters that concern the nation as a whole. However, in most cases, the central, or federal, government is restricted by the nation's constitution from taking over the powers that belong to the states.

To a large extent, the success or failure of a federal system depends on a nation's stability. In a number of

History Speaks

Nelson Rockefeller on Federalism

In 1962, Republican Nelson A. Rockefeller, then governor of New York State, described how a federal system works. He noted the sharing of power between the national government and state governments. Rockefeller later served as vice president under Gerald R. Ford (1974–1977).

By providing several sources of political strength and creativity, a federal system invites leadership—on all levels—to work toward genuine solutions to the problems of a diverse and complex society. These problems—whether they concern civil rights or urban development, industrialization or automation, natural resources or transportation—never arise at the same instant and in the same way throughout a great nation. A federal system, however, allows these problems to be met at the time and in the area where they first arise. If local solutions are not forthcoming, it is still possible to bring to bear the influence, the power, and the leadership of either the state or the national government.

developing countries, a federal system has failed to survive. Often, such countries have established unitary governmental systems in which all power is centralized, rather than federal systems, to better control disputing groups within the country.

ADVANTAGES OF A FEDERAL SYSTEM

A major advantage of a federal system of government is that it provides unity for the nation but still allows regional units, such as states, to have authority to handle local problems. In this way, a federal government is able to handle national affairs, while local matters are dealt with through local governments that are closer to the people.

A second advantage of a federal system is that local officials, who are elected by local voters, must be responsive to the needs of the people who elect them or else they may not be reelected. In contrast, in many unitary systems, officials of the national government, who are not actually responsible to the local people, operate the local government. Often, these officials are not as responsive to local needs. Thus, a federal system may result in a close relationship between the government and the people. In turn, this tends to make the government more responsive to local needs.

A third advantage is that a federal system provides overall unity for a country. In addition, the central government can devote its time and energy to national affairs, leaving local concerns to state and local governments.

DISADVANTAGES OF A FEDERAL SYSTEM

As with every type of government, a federal system has some disadvantages. One is that the system can produce a degree of duplication. Each state or province usually has an executive, a legislature, and a system of courts. On some occasions, the operation of state and local governments may duplicate the activities of the national government. This is true, for example, in the field of law enforcement, where a criminal may commit a crime that violates both state and national law. Duplication of effort in a federal system may cause some inefficiency and perhaps result in higher taxes to support the different levels of government.

Another disadvantage is that, while there may be uniformity of national law throughout the country, local laws and local governmental services may vary from one state to another. For example, traffic laws may vary from state to state. Certain actions may be legal in one state and illegal in others. Furthermore, the types of public services that are provided by state and local governments may differ considerably from one region to another.

In addition, disputes over who has power in certain areas may arise. For example, a dispute may arise over whether state or federal officials should investigate a crime or over bodies of water that are shared by states.

Thus, despite some disadvantages and the possibility of duplication, federal systems of government allow power and authority to be shared between different levels of government. Overall, in developed nations, such as the United States, a federalist system provides a stable and satisfactory type of government, one that is able to provide for the needs of the people and successfully interact with other nations.

See also: Constitutional Convention; Shared Powers.

FURTHER READING

Genovese, Michael A., and Lori Cox Han. *Encyclopedia of American Government and Civics.* New York: Facts On File, 2008.

Federalist, The

Also known as *The Federalist Papers*, a collection of 85 letters to the public in which the writers argued in favor of the **ratification** of the Constitution. The articles, written by Alexander Hamilton, James Madison (1809–1817), and John Jay, appeared in New York City newspapers beginning in October 1787. The essays probably had only a small impact on the ratification of the Constitution. However, they later gained importance as a classic statement of the **federal** philosophy underlying the Constitution.

BACKGROUND

The idea for *The Federalist* came from Alexander Hamilton, who wanted to wage a literary fight to explain the proposed Constitution and build support for it. Two of his fellow delegates to the Constitutional Convention of 1787, James Madison and John Jay, agreed to work with him. The first letter was published on October 27,

1787. In all, the newspapers published a series of 85 letters between October 1787 and August 1788. Of these, Hamilton wrote 56; Madison, 21; and Jay, 5. Hamilton and Madison collaborated on three. A serious illness in fall 1787 caused Jay's low output.

All of the letters bore the signature "Publius," a pseudonym—false name—adopted by the three authors. The name was chosen in honor of the ancient Roman statesman Publius Valerius Publicola. His last name translates as "friend of the people," and he played a key role in deposing Rome's last king and helping to establish the Roman Republic.

TOPICS COVERED

Federalist No. 1 listed six main topics as the subjects of the subsequent articles. These included the advantages of political union for the states, the weaknesses of the Articles of Confederation, the necessity for a strong federal government, how the proposed Constitution expressed the true principles of **republican** government, and similarities between the proposed Constitution and existing state constitutions. It also explained how adopting the Constitution would preserve republican government, liberty, and prosperity. In the end, the last two topics were discussed only briefly.

Two of the most noted of the letters are *Federalist No. 10* and *Federalist No. 84. Federalist No. 10* warns of the dangers of "factions," or interest groups. James Madison, the author of the essay, cautioned that **factions** would pursue their own interests,

History Speaks

James Madison and The Federalist No. 10

*T*he Federalist is a series of essays written by Alexander Hamilton, James Madison, and John Jay to support the ratification of the Constitution. Today, it provides historians and political scientists with keen insights into the Framers' thinking at the time. This excerpt from *Federalist No. 10*, written by James Madison and published in 1787, discusses factions.

No man is allowed to be a judge in his own cause, because his interest would certainly bias his judgment, and, not improbably, corrupt his integrity. With equal, nay with greater reason, a body of men are unfit to be both judges and parties at the same time; yet what are many of the most important acts of legislation, but so many judicial determinations, not indeed concerning the rights of single persons, but concerning the rights of large bodies of citizens? And what are the different classes of legislators but advocates and parties to the causes which they determine? . . .

It is in vain to say that enlightened statesmen will be able to adjust these clashing interests, and render them all subservient to the public good. Enlightened statesmen will not always be at the helm. Nor, in many cases, can such an adjustment be made at all without taking into view indirect and remote considerations, which will rarely prevail over the immediate interest which one party may find in disregarding the rights of another or the good of the whole.

The inference to which we are brought is, that the *causes* of faction cannot be removed, and that relief is only to be sought in the means of controlling its *effects*.

D–F

regardless of the rights of others or the will of the majority of the people. He argued that factions would exercise much more political power in smaller republics, such as the individual states, than they would in a larger republic. According to Madison, adopting a Constitution that bound the states together in a larger union would thus reduce the influence of factions.

Federalist No. 84, authored by Hamilton, is best known for outlining arguments against including a Bill of Rights in the proposed Constitution. He claimed that a Bill of Rights was not only unnecessary but also potentially dangerous to individual liberties. Hamilton suggested that later governments might consider liberties listed in a Bill of Rights to be the only rights enjoyed by the people.

As historian Clinton Rossiter wrote in an introduction to the papers: "*The Federalist* is the most important work in political science that has ever been written, or is likely ever to be written, in the United States. It is, indeed, the one product of the American mind that is rightly counted among the classics of political theory.... *The Federalist* stands third only to the Declaration of Independence and the Constitution itself among all the sacred writing of American political history."

See also: Articles of Confederation; Hamilton, Alexander.

FURTHER READING
Hamilton, Alexander, James Madison, and John Jay. Edited by Clinton Rossiter. *The Federalist Papers.* New York: Signet Classics, 2003.

Franklin, Benjamin

See Albany Plan of Union.

G–L

Gibbons v. Ogden *(1824)*

Landmark Supreme Court case that helped determine the supremacy of the **federal** government over the states with regard to **commerce** under the Commerce Clause of the Constitution. At the Constitutional Convention in 1787, the **Founders** recognized the importance of laws concerning interstate and foreign commerce. The Commerce Clause that they wrote into the Constitution gave Congress broad powers to regulate commerce.

In time, the federal government's power over interstate commerce became one of its most important powers. However, in the first years of the nation's history, that power was used so rarely that there was no need to define precisely what was meant by commerce "among the several States."

Not until 35 years after the **ratification** of the Constitution did a case involving the scope of this power come before the Supreme Court.

THE CASE
The circumstances leading to the Supreme Court's decision in the case of *Gibbons v. Ogden* involved a dispute over a **monopoly** of steamboat operations between New York and New Jersey. Other states fought this monopoly by closing their waters to ships operating under the monopoly. They also granted steamship monopolies of their own. The result was chaos on the nation's rivers and harbors.

The case that broke the monopoly involved Aaron Ogden, a former New Jersey governor, and his partner, Thomas Gibbons, who ran a steam-driven ferry between New Jersey and

New York City. In 1815, Ogden had acquired a license from the New York monopoly, and Gibbons held a permit under a federal coastal act for his two boats. Despite their partnership, Gibbons ran his boats to New York in defiance of Ogden's monopoly rights. In 1819, Ogden sued for an **injunction** to stop Gibbons's infringement of his rights under the monopoly. New York courts ordered Gibbons to halt his ferry service. Gibbons appealed to the Supreme Court, arguing that his federal license took precedence over the state-granted monopoly license. He believed that he should be allowed to continue his ferrying in New York waters.

THE DECISION

The Supreme Court considered two basic questions. Did Congress have power under the commerce clause to regulate navigation? If so, did Congress have exclusive power to regulate it, or did the states also have power to regulate commerce? Delivering the Court's opinion on March 2, 1824, Chief Justice John Marshall answered the first question by refusing to interpret the federal commerce power narrowly or to omit navigation from its scope. Concerning the second question, Marshall said that the commerce power of Congress applied to commerce with foreign nations as well as to commerce among the states. However, Marshall did not find that the commerce power prohibited all state regulation.

Settling Two Key Issues Marshall's opinion settled two points—first, that navigation was commerce and, second, that where state exercise of its power conflicts with federal exercise of the commerce power, the state must give way. Thus, Marshall asserted the supreme power of the national government within the federal system.

In making the second point, Marshall laid the groundwork for extending the commerce power to other forms of transportation and communications. By leaving the power to regulate wholly internal commerce to the states only so long as that commerce did not "extend to or affect" other states, he planted the idea that would later allow Congress to regulate the manufacture of goods and matters that themselves were not in commerce but would affect interstate commerce.

Extending the Power of Congress Congress did not make much use of the power claimed for it by *Gibbons v. Ogden* until later in the 1800s. Between 1824, when *Gibbons v. Ogden* was decided, and the 1880s, when a need arose for federal regulation of the nation's railroads and interstate corporations, the Court's rulings on the commerce power focused on determining when state actions on commerce were unconstitutional.

See also: McCulloch v. Maryland (1819).

FURTHER READING

Cox, Thomas H. *Gibbons v. Ogden, Law, and Society in the Early Republic.* Athens: Ohio University Press, 2009.

Levinson, Isabel Simone. *Gibbons V. Ogden: Controlling Trade Between States.* Berkeley Heights, N.J.: Enslow, 1999.

Hamilton, Alexander (1755–1804)

One of the nation's key **Founders**, first secretary of the Treasury, and co-author of *The Federalist,* a series of essays in support of the Constitution. Hamilton supported a strong central government.

EARLY LIFE

Alexander Hamilton, the illegitimate son of James A. Hamilton and Rachel Fawcett Lavien, was born on the island Nevis in the British West Indies. Most historians place the date as January 11, 1755. Other sources say 1757.

James abandoned Rachel in 1765, after they moved to St. Croix, another island in the Caribbean. In his father's absence, Alexander became a clerk at a trading post to earn money. The economy of St. Croix was largely based on sugar plantations using slave labor. Historians suggest that this early experience had a number of effects on Hamilton's later life. His exposure to business gave him a keen mind for trade and made him good with accounts and numbers. Having seen a number of slave revolts brutally crushed, he became a lifelong opponent of slavery. Unlike the rest of the Founders, Hamilton spent his formative years outside of the colonies. Thus, he never developed the regional loyalties that so many of his compatriots held.

MOVE TO THE THIRTEEN COLONIES

By age 17, Hamilton yearned to leave St. Croix and explore the world. He had proven himself an intelligent young man and fine writer. When a letter of his was printed in the St. Croix newspaper, a local clergyman, Hugh Knox, decided that Hamilton deserved to be sent overseas for a college education. Knox took up a collection, and Hamilton was sent to a school in Elizabethtown, New Jersey, in 1772.

After attending college prep school in New Jersey, Hamilton attended King's College, now Columbia University, in New York City. Hamilton quickly became a **Patriot** for the revolutionary cause. In response to a series of pro-British pamphlets written by Samuel Seabury, Hamilton wrote *A Full Vindication of the measures of Congress* and *The Farmer Refuted.* He was around 20 years old at the time.

Like those of Thomas Jefferson, Hamilton's arguments for liberty and revolution were founded on seventeenth-century **Enlightenment** philosopher John Locke and his doctrine of natural rights. Natural rights, unlike legal rights, are considerations due to every person by virtue of their existence. As such rights are not given, it is always a crime when they are taken away.

Unlike Jefferson, however, Hamilton's original solution to the problem of liberty in the colonies was to bring **Great Britain** and the colonies closer together. If the colonies were given more power and autonomy, they could be equal partners in the empire, ensuring that the colonists were not abused by the king. Britain, however, proved unwilling to give the colonies any power.

ROLE IN THE REVOLUTION

In 1775, Hamilton joined the New York militia to fight against the British. A lieutenant, he led a successful raid against a British artillery position. After the attack, Hamilton's company became an artillery company. Eventually, Hamilton was invited to become General George Washington's aide. This association with Washington introduced him to a number of influential revolutionaries. It also gave Hamilton a new perspective on the Continental Congress, as he was able to see firsthand how their internal struggles were affecting the military. **Factionalism** within the Congress kept them from properly supplying the troops, and Hamilton never forgot it.

Serving in the Congress Following the passage of the Articles of Confederation in 1781 by the Second Continental Congress, Hamilton was elected to the new Congress of the Confederation as the representative from New York. There, he sought to fix the problems he had seen during wartime. Namely, the Continental Congress had been unable to supply the military because it had been unable to collect taxes. The weak **federal** government under the Articles was overruled by the individual states, and thus had no power to impose taxes. The first attempt to fix this was by imposing a 5 percent tax on imported goods. The measure required approval by all the states, but Rhode Island and Virginia voted it down.

Plan to Revise the Articles As the country continued to struggle with its finances, its soldiers continued to demand the pay they were owed for their years of service. Angry mobs began to organize. Congress was forced to flee from Philadelphia to Princeton, New Jersey. Hamilton had foreseen these problems and was continually frustrated both by Congress and by the states' refusal to pay for anything that benefited the nation as a whole. While in Princeton, he wrote a proposal to reform the Articles of Confederation. His reforms would strengthen the federal government significantly and give it the power to levy taxes. He also called for a separation of power into the three branches of government that exist in the United States today.

CONVENTION DELEGATE

As a delegate to the Constitutional Convention in 1787, Hamilton continued to call for a strong central government. Many of the other delegates felt that his plan was too close to a **monarchy,** and his suggestions were largely ignored. His proposals would have almost eliminated the individual states, and he would have allowed the president to remain in office for life, barring corruption. While Hamilton's draft of the Constitution differed from the final form presented to the Congress, he voted for it anyway. It was much stronger and provided a more powerful central government than the Articles of Confederation.

After Congress approved the draft, Hamilton, John Jay, and James Madison wrote *The Federalist,* a series of essays first published in newspapers, to convince the country to ratify it. Hamilton wrote a majority of the articles in *The Federalist*, and today they comprise the primary source, other than the U.S. Constitution itself, by which lawyers and judges interpret the Constitution. The breadth of his defense marks Hamilton as one of the Constitution's greatest defenders.

See also: *Federalist, The*; Jefferson, Thomas; Loose Constructionist; Strict Constructionist.

FURTHER READING

Ambrose, Douglas, and Robert Martin. *The Many Faces of Alexander Hamilton: The Life and Legacy of American's Most Elusive Founding Father.* New York: NYU Press, 2007.

Brookhiser, Richard. *Alexander Hamilton, American.* New York: Free Press, 2000.

Henry, Patrick (1736–1799)

American revolutionary, orator, and one of the nation's **Founders**, a fiery politician who greatly influenced the thirteen colonies' move toward independence. Henry was an early supporter of colonial independence but grew suspicious of the later move to a strong central government, fearful that the **federalist** system would not work.

EARLY LIFE

Henry was born in Studley, Virginia, on May 29, 1736. His father, John, was an immigrant from Scotland who married Sarah Winston Syme, a widow from an important family in Hanover County, Virginia. The Henrys were landed gentry, although they were not in the upper ranks of the **aristocracy**.

Patrick was schooled at home. His father gave him a classical education that included reading Latin. Young Patrick taught himself law and passed the bar in 1760. Henry's most famous case came in 1763. The "Parson's Cause" was a suit filed by Reverend James Maury (1719–1769) against Louisa County in Virginia. The **colonial** government had paid local clergy in tobacco, and for many years, the price of tobacco had remained the same: two cents per pound. Because of a drought, the price spiked, but Virginia passed a law stating that any contracts paid in tobacco would be paid at the regular rate. The clergy were angered and complained to England, which overturned Virginia's law.

Reverend Maury then sued his local county for back pay. He won his case. All that was left was to determine what that back pay would be. Louisa County called in Patrick Henry to argue on its behalf, and because of Henry's fiery speech, Maury was awarded a single penny. Henry denounced the clergy and claimed that any king who would overturn the laws of a freely elected government was nothing more than a tyrant. His revolutionary sentiments made him popular with the people.

ELECTION TO THE VIRGINIA LEGISLATURE

In 1765, Henry was elected to the House of Burgesses, the colonial government of Virginia. Here, his radical politics started to upset the most conservative members. When the members who were most loyal to the British king were away, Henry proposed the Virginia Stamp Act Resolutions. The Resolutions claimed that under British law the government had no right to impose the taxes in the Stamp Act unless those being taxed had representation in Parliament.

After an impassioned speech and cries of treason against Henry, the Resolutions went to a vote and narrowly passed. They were later printed and distributed throughout the colonies. Henry's Resolutions stirred public anger, which resulted in the Stamp Act riots, pushing the colonies closer to revolution.

Henry gave his most remembered speech before the House of Burgesses on March 23, 1775. The colonies were on the brink of revolution and Virginia needed to decide whether or not it was going to send troops to face the British. Henry's words, as reported in an 1817 biography, are remembered to this day:

> Is life so dear, or peace so sweet, as to be purchased at the price of chains and slavery? Forbid it, Almighty God! I know not what course others may take; but as for me, *give me liberty or give me death!*

LATER ROLE
Before the outbreak of the American Revolution (1775–1783), Henry was a delegate to the First Continental Congress in 1774,

although he accomplished little of note. He had increasingly little to do with his fellow revolutionaries as time went on. Henry did not believe in a strong central government, and he therefore declined to attend the Constitutional Convention in 1787. He believed that too great a focus on the nation as a whole would cause the government to lose sight of matters concerning the individual states. He disliked the government's increasing focus on helping the industrial North, as his concerns were with the **agrarian** South. Henry later urged his fellow Virginians to vote down the Constitution.

Although the fiery orator Patrick Henry strongly favored independence from Great Britain in 1776, he later opposed the U.S. Constitution. He feared that the federal system it established made the national government too powerful.

He claimed, for example, that **federal** tax collectors would harass good, working citizens. In addition, he believed that the president would be a worse ruler than the king had been. Following the **ratification** of the Constitution in 1788, Henry retired from public life. He died on June 6, 1799, in Red Hill, Virginia.

See also: States' Rights.

FURTHER READING

Mayer, Henry. *A Son of Thunder: Patrick Henry and the American Republic*. Jackson, Tenn.: Grove Press, 2001.

Vaughan, David J. *Give Me Liberty: The Uncompromising Statesmanship of Patrick Henry*. Nashville, Tenn.: Cumberland House Publishing, 2002.

Jackson, Andrew (1767–1845)

War hero and seventh president of the United States (1829–1837). Andrew Jackson was nicknamed "Old Hickory" because people thought he was as tough as hickory wood. His military fame made him a national hero and ultimately led to his election to the presidency in 1828. Although a Southerner and a slaveholder, Andrew Jackson supported the national government and the Union of the states above all. Jackson expanded the power of the presidency unlike any of his predecessors.

EARLY LIFE

Andrew Jackson was born to Andrew and Elizabeth Jackson on March 15, 1767, on the border between North and South Carolina, an area called Waxhaws. His father died before he was born. He was the youngest of three sons. Jackson, a teenager during the Revolutionary War (1775–1783), joined the Continental Army at the age of 13. He and his brother Robert were captured by the British and held as prisoners of war. While a captive, Andrew was ordered to polish the boots of a British soldier. When he refused, the soldier slashed him with his sword, leaving Jackson with a permanent scar and a lifelong hatred of the British. Both Robert and Andrew's oldest brother, Hugh, died during the war. At age 14, Jackson was left an orphan after his mother died.

Following the war, Jackson worked briefly in a saddle shop, then as a teacher. In 1784, he decided to take up law and moved to Salisbury, North Carolina, to study. He was admitted to the bar in 1787 and became a prosecutor in Nashville, which was still a part of North Carolina at the time.

ENTERING POLITICS

In 1796, Tennessee became a state, and Andrew Jackson was elected to the **House of Representatives**. He was then elected as a senator in 1797, but he resigned his post before serving out a full year. Jackson returned to Tennessee in 1798 and became a judge in the state supreme court.

CREEK WAR

Jackson led two successful military campaigns that helped make him a national hero. The first took place on the frontier of what is now Alabama. As a colonel in the Tennessee militia, Jackson led an attack against the

Red Stick Creek tribe and their leader, Tecumseh, at the Battle of Horseshoe Bend in Alabama. The United States was at war with the Creek to gain their land. As a result of the battle, Jackson secured a treaty granting 23 million acres (9,307,769 hectares) to the United States for settlement. He was also promoted to major general.

BATTLE OF NEW ORLEANS

The second battle that brought Jackson wide acclaim was the 1815 Battle of New Orleans, the last battle of the War of 1812 (1812–1814) against the British. Although the Treaty of Ghent had been signed in December 1814, news of the peace treaty did not reach America because of the slow methods of communication at the time. Thus, the British attacked the port city of New Orleans, Louisiana, on January 8, 1815.

The Americans, under Jackson's command, numbered 5,000. They took only minor casualties but defeated 7,500 trained British soldiers. The British experienced heavy losses, with more than 2,000 dead or missing. Jackson won a decisive victory, becoming a national hero.

TO THE WHITE HOUSE

Jackson was elected senator from Tennessee in 1822. The state legislature nominated him as a candidate for president in the upcoming election of 1824. In the election, Jackson ran against William H. Crawford, John Quincy Adams, and Henry Clay. Jackson received the most **electoral votes,** but because the votes were split among four candidates, he did not get a majority, or more than 50 percent, of the vote. Under the terms of the U.S. Constitution, the election was decided by the House of Representatives. The House elected John Quincy Adams (1825–1829). Many voters were outraged and declared it

BORN TO COMMAND.

OF VETO MEMORY.

HAD I BEEN CONSULTED.

KING ANDREW THE FIRST.

In the 1830s, a political cartoonist represented the opposing Whig Party's view of President Andrew Jackson as a king trying to destroy the U.S. Constitution, which is the basis of America's federal system of government.

the "Stolen Election." The popular outrage that Jackson, a man of the people, had been robbed of the office helped secure his election in 1828.

Jackson's presidency was remarkable because of his expansion of executive, or presidential, power. He was the first president to make use of the **pocket veto.** According to the Constitution, if a bill passed by Congress is not signed into law by the president before the Congress goes into recess, then the bill is dead. Jackson also made use of the regular **veto** more than all the presidents before him combined.

INCREASING PRESIDENTIAL POWER

Jackson also employed the idea of "rotation in office" to **federal** employees, believing that no one should remain in government bureaucracy for a lengthy period of time. In reality, Jackson's version of rotation in office meant giving government jobs to his friends and party supporters. It was the beginning of the **spoils system,** in which political cronies, or buddies, receive rewards for their support after an election.

Jackson extended his power over the economy by opposing the Second Bank of the United States. During his presidency, the bank's charter came up for renewal. He opposed the bank because he believed that it only enriched the wealthy and Northeastern business owners. Jackson withdrew federal funds from the bank even before the charter expired, and he vetoed the bill to renew the bank. Congress did not have enough votes to override his veto.

Unlike any president before him, Jackson claimed to speak for the common people, and he used this sense of popular support to impose his will on the country's affairs. With his use of the veto, he was able to significantly increase the power of the presidency. Indeed, presidential powers have continued to expand since Jackson's time.

See also: Adams, John Quincy; Calhoun, John C.; Clay, Henry.

FURTHER READING

Brands, H.W. *Andrew Jackson: His Life and Times.* New York: Anchor Books, 2006.

Marrin, Albert. *Old Hickory: Andrew Jackson and the American People.* New York: Dutton Juvenile, 2004.

Meacham, Jon. *American Lion: Andrew Jackson in the White House.* New York: Random House, 2008.

Remini, Robert V. *Andrew Jackson.* New York: Palgrave Macmillan, 2008.

Jefferson, Thomas (1743–1826)

Author of the Declaration of Independence (1776), one of the nation's most brilliant **Founders**, and third president of the United States (1801–1809). In the Declaration, Jefferson established the principle "that all men are created equal." As president, he worked to maintain the balance of federalism—shared responsibility between the states and the national government.

A strict constructionist, Jefferson believed that the **federal** government held only those powers granted to it by the Constitution. Yet, when he had the opportunity to buy the vast Louisiana Territory from France, he quickly concluded the purchase—although the Constitution did not specifically grant the government the power to buy land.

EARLY LIFE

Thomas Jefferson was born on April 13, 1743, in Shadwell, Virginia, to Peter Jefferson and Jane Randolph. Both were from wealthy families, and young Jefferson enjoyed a privileged upbringing. He started school in 1752 and received a classical education that included Latin, Greek, and French.

In 1760, Jefferson was admitted to the College of William and Mary. He wasted his first year at the college partying and attending horse races. Jefferson quickly came to regret this wasted time, and when he returned for a second year, he paid much closer attention to his studies. He became friends with William Small, a professor at the college who treated him like a son. Jefferson was introduced to Governor Francis Fauquier, who was so impressed with Jefferson that he invited him to weekly dinners at the governor's mansion. The dinners consisted of music and spirited, intellectual conversation that introduced young Jefferson to the ideas and ideals of the **Enlightenment.** His personal and political beliefs were forever changed, and he spent his life working on behalf of enlightened beliefs and progress.

From 1762 to 1767, he studied law under George Wythe, a famous lawyer. Jefferson passed the bar in 1767 and began practicing law in Williamsburg. He handled more than 100 cases during his career.

ENTERING POLITICS

In 1768, Jefferson began construction on his home, Monticello, on a mountaintop near Shadwell, Virginia. He also ran for election to the House of Burgesses, the governing body of Virginia. In 1769, Jefferson joined the House of Burgesses as a representative from Albemarle County, thus beginning his long political career.

In 1772, Jefferson married Martha Wayles Skelton, who came from a wealthy family. Her **dowry** doubled Jefferson's land holdings. Together, they had six children.

At the time Jefferson entered politics, the British Parliament had just passed the Coercive Acts. These acts were a response to the Boston Tea Party, in which Massachusetts colonists, disguised as Native Americans, threw 342 chests of tea into Boston Harbor to protest the new British taxes on tea. The Coercive Acts consisted of the Boston Port Act, the Massachusetts Government Act, the Administration of Justice Act, the Quartering Act, and the Quebec Act.

Altogether, these acts punished the colonists, by creating greater intrusions into the governance and daily lives of citizens than ever before. Colonists could be forced to travel to far-flung colonies or even **Great Britain** to testify at trials, depriving them of their livelihoods. They were forced to house and feed British soldiers. In addition, all

G–L

government officials in Massachusetts were to be British appointees.

RIGHTS AND LIBERTIES

The colonists were outraged and took the acts as a sign that the British government could and would take away all liberties in the colonies if it so chose. Jefferson's first great piece of political writing was a response to these acts. *A Summary View of the Rights of British America* was published in 1774. It took on a different line of argument than previous resolutions against the acts. Jefferson argued that the colonists had **natural rights** to self-governance.

The idea of natural rights is a philosophical concept; proponents believe that humans, by virtue of their existence, are entitled to certain considerations and treatment. People are owed these rights, regardless of circumstance. By contrast, rights granted by law can be altered or taken away.

WIDESPREAD FAME

Jefferson's arguments in *A Summary View* brought him fame throughout the colonies. His support for independence and natural expressiveness made him a perfect choice for the Second Continental Congress. Virginia elected him as its delegate in 1775. Ironically, Jefferson arrived in Philadelphia for the Congress with three of his slaves.

WRITING THE DECLARATION

At the Continental Congress, Jefferson was usually quiet and shy. While others, such as John Adams, offered robust debate, Jefferson watched and wrote. He wrote many resolutions for the Congress, and this gave him a reputation as a skilled essayist. When it came time to write the Declaration of Independence, Jefferson was chosen along with Benjamin Franklin, John Adams, Roger Sherman, and Robert Livingston to form the drafting committee.

While the other members of the committee had input on the first draft, the form and content was entirely Jefferson's. Indeed, it was his greatest contribution to the American Revolution (1775–1783) and to history. His belief in natural rights, first discussed in *A Summary View*, became the central idea of the Declaration and the moral ground upon which the Revolution rested. At the time of its writing, Jefferson did not believe he had done any original work. He was merely expressing beliefs that all Americans held. Nor was the Declaration considered his work, but rather the work of the committee. It is only in hindsight that the Declaration is considered the most powerful example of his brilliant and passionate mind.

See also: Adams, John; Elastic Clause; Virginia and Kentucky Resolutions.

FURTHER READING

Behrman, Carol H. *Thomas Jefferson.* Minneapolis, Minn.: Lerner Publications, 2004.

Bernstein, R.B. *Thomas Jefferson.* New York: Oxford University Press, 2005.

Hayes, Kevin J. *The Road to Monticello: The Life and Mind of Thomas Jefferson.* New York: Oxford University Press, 2008.

Jones, Veda Boyd. *Thomas Jefferson: Author of the Declaration of Independence.* New York: Chelsea House, 2000.

Loose Constructionist

One who believes the U.S. Constitution should be interpreted loosely, or broadly. Loose constructionists have argued that the authors of the Constitution meant for the Constitution to adapt itself to the changing needs of the country. They believe that there are things implied by or simply understood by the wording of the Constitution. They further believe that it is the job of the Supreme Court to clarify any vague language in laws and to interpret the Constitution in the most practical way possible. Over time, the loose constructionist interpretation of the Constitution allowed the **federal** government to increase its power.

Loose constructionists maintain that the Constitution grants the federal government the power to enact any laws that are deemed necessary for the general welfare of the nation. This view was the basic philosophy of the Federalists, including Alexander Hamilton and George Washington (1789–1797), who argued for a strong central government with numerous powers over the states.

DIFFERING VIEWS

In contrast to loose constructionists, strict constructionists believe that the Constitution should be interpreted strictly, or literally, and that only the original intentions of its authors should be considered. Strict constructionists assert that the federal government can only exercise the powers that are clearly spelled out by the Constitution and that all other powers belong to the states or the people.

In 1791, one of the first disputes between strict constructionists and loose constructionists took place, when Secretary of the Treasury Alexander Hamilton proposed establishing the First Bank of the United States. Hamilton's bank bill was to establish a national bank that would collect taxes, hold government money, and make loans to the government and borrowers. It would also create a standard form of currency, because at the time each state had its own form of currency. President George Washington asked for a written opinion from all his cabinet members about the bill.

OPPOSING VIEWS

Taking the strict constructionist position, Secretary of State Thomas Jefferson insisted that a national bank was unconstitutional because the Constitution did not specifically give Congress the power to create a bank. However, Alexander Hamilton took the loose constructionist position. He pointed out that because of the wording of the Constitution, some issues would clearly be within the power of the federal government, some would not be, and some would "leave room for controversy and difference of opinion, and concerning which a reasonable latitude of judgment must be allowed." Hamilton interpreted the Constitution to mean that because it delegated certain specified powers to the federal government, this implied that the federal government also had the power to enact laws that would be useful in carrying out these powers. George Washington, persuaded by

G–
L

Hamilton's argument, signed the bank bill into law in April 1791.

THE ISSUE TODAY

Today, there is still an ongoing debate in the United States concerning how the Supreme Court should interpret the Constitution. Strict constructionists believe that judges must always interpret the Constitution as the authors intended. Loose constructionists, however, believe that the Constitution is a "living document" that must be adapted to contemporary circumstances, ones that the Founding Fathers could not have foreseen.

See also: Hamilton, Alexander; Jefferson, Thomas; Strict Constructionists; Washington, George.

FURTHER READING

Kluge, Dave. *The People's Guide to the United States Constitution*. Glendale, Calif.: Action Publishing, 2007.

Schultz, David. *Encyclopedia of the U.S. Constitution*. New York: Facts On File, 2009.

M–R

Madison, James

See Constitutional Convention.

Marshall, John (1755–1835)

Fourth Chief Justice of the United States whose strong Court opinions in the early 1800s helped strengthen the **federal** government at the expense of the states. Marshall, a fervent Federalist, was nominated by President John Adams (1797–1801) and served until his death in 1835.

EARLY LIFE

The first of 15 children, John Marshall was born in a log cabin on the Virginia frontier near Germantown. His father, Thomas Marshall, descended from Welsh immigrants, was an assistant surveyor to George Washington and a member of the Virginia House of Burgesses. His mother, Mary Randolph Keith Marshall, was the daughter of a Scottish clergyman.

During the Revolutionary War (1775–1783), young Marshall participated in the siege of Norfolk as a member of the Culpeper Minute Men and was present at Brandywine, Monmouth, Stony Point, and Valley Forge as a member of the third Virginia Regiment. In 1779, he returned home to await a new assignment but was never recalled. He left the Continental Army with the rank of captain in 1781.

POLITICS AND LAW

Marshall's only formal training in the law came in 1780 when he attended a series of law lectures at the College of William and Mary. Marshall was elected to the Virginia House of Delegates from Fauquier County in 1782 and 1784. He reentered the House of Delegates in 1787 and was influential in Virginia's **ratification** of the new U.S. Constitution. At the state ratifying convention, his main concern was the need for **judicial review.** By

1789, Marshall was considered to be a leading Federalist in his state.

Marshall refused many appointments in the Federalist administrations of George Washington (1789–1797) and John Adams. In 1799, however, Washington persuaded Marshall to run for the U.S. **House of Representatives** as a Federalist from Richmond. His career in the House was brief, however, for in 1800 he became secretary of state under Adams. Then in September 1800, Chief Justice Oliver Ellsworth resigned, and Adams nominated Marshall to the Court.

CHIEF JUSTICE

As the primary founder of the nation's system of constitutional law, including the doctrine of judicial review, Marshall participated in more than 1,000 Supreme Court decisions, writing more than 500 of them himself. In 1807, he presided over the treason trial of former Vice President Aaron Burr, angering President Thomas Jefferson (1801–1809), who sought Burr's conviction. Burr was acquitted.

In 1831, at age 76, Marshall underwent successful surgery in Philadelphia for the removal of kidney stones. Three years later, he developed an enlarged liver, and his health declined rapidly. Marshall died on July 6, 1835, three months short of his 80th birthday. Some like to tell the story that the Liberty Bell in Philadelphia cracked as it tolled in mourning.

See also: Adams, John; Federalist System; *Gibbons v. Ogden* (1824); *McCulloch v. Maryland* (1819).

FURTHER READING

Simon, James F. *What Kind of Nation: Thomas Jefferson, John Marshall, and the Epic Struggle to Create a United States.* New York: Simon & Schuster, 2003.

McCulloch v. Maryland *(1819)*

Landmark Supreme Court case that established the supremacy of national laws, passed by Congress, over state laws. *McCulloch v. Maryland* is one of the most important cases in American constitutional law and key to the nation's **federal** system of government.

THE ISSUE OF THE BANK OF THE UNITED STATES

In 1790, Alexander Hamilton, George Washington's (1789–1797) secretary of the Treasury, proposed the establishment of a national banking system. The U.S. Constitution did not expressly grant the national government the power to do so. Hamilton, who interpreted the Constitution loosely, argued that the power was implied and that the bank was "necessary and proper" to carry out the expressed financial powers of the national government.

Thomas Jefferson (1801–1809), a strict constructionist, opposed the bank, claiming it was a threat to the states' control of their local economies. He also believed that the bank was unconstitutional, noting that the Constitution did not grant Congress the power to establish a bank. He further argued that it "does not stand

M–R

on the degree of *necessity* that can honestly justify it."

President Washington supported Hamilton, and Congress established the Bank of the United States in 1791. A branch of the bank was set up later in Baltimore. The Maryland legislature tried to cripple the bank by imposing a tax on it. James McCulloch, the chief cashier of the Baltimore branch, refused to pay the tax. Maryland then convicted McCulloch for refusing to pay the tax. The case

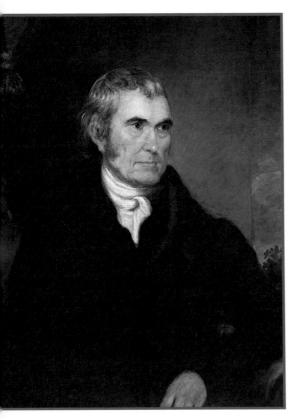

As the chief justice of the United States from 1801 until 1835, John Marshall strengthened the power of the national government through landmark rulings such as *McCulloch v. Maryland* and *Gibbons v. Ogden*.

eventually reached the U.S. Supreme Court.

THE CASE

McCulloch's lawyers—loose constructionists—agreed that the power to create a bank was not an expressed power of the national government. Nevertheless, they argued, Congress had the power to create a national bank as an appropriate way to exercise the **enumerated powers** of collecting taxes, borrowing money, and caring for U.S. property. McCulloch's lawyers also argued that although the power to tax was reserved to the states, states could not use that power in a way that would interfere with the operation of the national government.

The lawyers representing the state of Maryland—strict constructionists—argued that the power to charter a bank was not an expressed power of the national government. They noted that the necessary and proper clause only gave Congress the power to pass laws that were absolutely necessary to the exercise of its enumerated powers. Because a bank was not absolutely necessary to exercise any of its enumerated powers, Congress had no authority to establish it. Maryland's lawyers also argued that the state had the right to tax the bank because the power to tax was reserved to the states and could be used as they saw fit.

THE DECISION

The Supreme Court unanimously rejected Maryland's arguments. Chief Justice John Marshall spoke for the

Court. First, Marshall considered the basic notion of the federal Union. Did the national government derive its power from the states, as the states' rights position held? Or were the powers of the Constitution derived from the people? Marshall defined the supremacy of the national government within the federal system:

> The government of the Union ... is emphatically and truly a government of the people. In form and in substance it emanates from them. Its powers are granted by them, and are to be exercised directly on them, for them benefit.... It can never be in their interest and cannot be presumed to have been their intention, to clog and embarrass its execution, by withholding the most appropriate means.

Next, Marshall addressed the question of the power of the national government to establish a bank. He took a loose constructionist position. Marshall admitted that the power to charter a bank was not among the enumerated powers of Congress. He held, however, that such a power could be inferred from the necessary and proper clause. He set forth his views on how the powers of the national government should be broadly interpreted, establishing the doctrine of **implied powers.**

> Let the end be legitimate, let it be within the scope of the Constitution, and all means which are appropriate, which are plainly assigned to that end, which are not prohibited, but consistent with the letter and spirit of the Constitution, are constitutional.

The Court then considered whether Maryland had the right to tax the bank. Marshall's opinion set forth the doctrine of national supremacy, which was based on the supremacy clause of Article 6 of the Constitution.

> If any one proposition could command the universal assent of mankind, we might expect that it would be this—that the government of the Union, though limited in its powers, is supreme within its sphere of action. Hence, no state possesses the power to retard, impede, burden, or in any manner control the operations of the constitutional laws passed by Congress.

Thus, the Supreme Court held the Maryland law to be unconstitutional.

SIGNIFICANCE OF THE RULING
The importance of *McCulloch v. Maryland* is enormous. In this case, the Supreme Court rejected the states' rights claim that the powers of the national government were derived from the states. The Court established the implied powers through a broad interpretation of the necessary and proper clause. In addition, it held that a state could not interfere with the legal activities of the national government. Thus, within the nation's federal system, the national government is supreme. A state constitution or law cannot conflict with

the U.S. Constitution, national laws, or treaties.

See also: Gibbons v. Ogden (1824); Hamilton, Alexander; Jefferson, Thomas; Loose Constructionists; States' Rights; Strict Constructionists.

FURTHER READING

Genovese, Michael A., and Lori Cox Han. *Encyclopedia of American Government and Civics.* New York: Facts On File, 2008.

Hartman, Gary L., Roy M. Mersky, and Cindy L. Tate. *Landmark Supreme Court Cases: The Most Influential Decisions of the Supreme Court of the United States.* New York: Checkmark Books, 2006.

Necessary and Proper Clause

See Elastic Clause.

New Federalism

A political philosophy that calls for the transfer of certain powers from the U.S. **federal** government to the states. A primary objective of New Federalism is to return to the states some of the power that was lost to the federal government in the mid-twentieth century. For example, as a consequence of President Franklin D. Roosevelt's (1933–1945) New Deal programs to fight the **Great Depression** of the 1930s, federal power over the economy increased significantly. In addition, the federal civil rights laws of the 1960s shifted a variety of powers concerning voting requirements and **integration** to the federal government. New Federalism relies on both a **federalist** tradition dating back to the founding of the country and on the Tenth Amendment.

RETURNING POWER TO THE STATES

In the late twentieth century, two presidents strongly advocated the idea of New Federalism—Richard M. Nixon (1969–1974) and Ronald Reagan (1981–1989). New Federalism usually involves the federal government providing block grants to the states to solve various social issues or concerns, such as housing or welfare. The federal government monitors the outcomes of the grants but provides little direction to the states on how the programs are to be implemented.

Advocates of this approach sometimes cite a quotation from a dissent by Louis Brandeis in the Supreme Court case *New State Ice Co. v. Liebmann* (1932):

> It is one of the happy incidents of the federal system that a single courageous state may, if its citizens choose, serve as a laboratory; and try novel social and economic experiments without risk to the rest of the country.

OPPOSITION

Opponents of New Federalism generally believe that the federal government, rather than the individual states, is better equipped to ensure equal treatment of all the nation's citizens. Critics contend that, among other things, New Federalism is a way to restore, at least in part, the unequal racist policies of the past.

See also: Block Grants; Nixon, Richard; Reagan, Ronald.

Nixon, Richard (1913–1994)

Thirty-seventh president of the United States (1969–1974). Although Richard Nixon ended direct American involvement in Vietnam and was known for his program of "New Federalism," his second term was tainted by his involvement in the 1972 Watergate scandal, which led to his resignation in 1974.

EARLY LIFE

Richard Milhous Nixon was born on January 9, 1913, in Yorba Linda, California. His parents, Francis and Hannah Nixon, were **Quakers** who lived a modest, even poor, life marked by financial woes and loss. He had four brothers, two of whom died before reaching adulthood.

An excellent student, Nixon graduated with honors from Whittier High School in Whittier, California. Although he was offered scholarships to Harvard and Yale, he could not afford the remaining costs of attending those universities and settled for Whittier College, a Quaker school. Nixon graduated from college with honors and went on to Duke University Law School. Duke offered him a full scholarship, and in 1937, he graduated third in his class. After passing the California bar exam, Nixon practiced law in Whittier until 1941, when the United States entered World War II (1939–1945). In 1938, he married Thelma "Pat" Ryan, and the two lived briefly in Washington, D.C.

Despite being eligible for exemption from military service because of his religion, Nixon decided to join the military. During the war, he served in the navy in the South Pacific. When the war ended, Nixon returned to his home in Whittier, where he and his wife started a family.

ENTERING POLITICS

In 1946, the Republicans in Whittier asked Nixon to run for the **House of Representatives**. He defeated a five-time **incumbent.** As part of his public service, Nixon and the other members of the Select Committee on Foreign Aid toured Europe in 1947. The trip proved that Nixon was adept in dealing with foreign nations, and he gained a reputation for being good with foreign policy.

However, it was as a member of the House Un-American Activities Committee that Nixon made a name for himself. The controversial committee worked to root out Communists from the **federal** government, and Nixon led a charge against Alger Hiss, a former State Department official believed at the time to have Communist ties. Ultimately, Hiss was convicted of **perjury** and served 44 months in prison. Unfortunately, the overzealous committee also damaged the lives and careers of many innocent Americans.

VICE PRESIDENT

Because of his growing reputation, Dwight D. Eisenhower (1953–1961) chose Richard Nixon as his vice-presidential running mate in the election of 1952. The Eisenhower/Nixon ticket won the election. As vice president, Nixon spent much of his time traveling the world, working to establish good foreign relations with other nations.

M–R

Nixon's service as vice president made him a natural choice for the Republican Party's candidate in the election of 1960. However, he narrowly lost to Democrat John F. Kennedy (1961–1963). Eight years later, however, Nixon again received the Republican Party's nomination. Nixon won the election over Democrat Hubert Humphrey and Independent George Wallace.

PRESIDENT NIXON

Richard M. Nixon came to power during the Vietnam War (1959–1975). The United States was divided over the war, angry with the seemingly endless fighting and bloodshed, and ready for its troops to come home. There was no easy solution to bring the war to a close, but Nixon encouraged negotiations with the North Vietnamese and started bringing American troops home. By 1973, he had brought most of the troops home, though it took two years longer than he had anticipated.

Following the end of the Vietnam War, Nixon wanted to focus on improving things at home. In his second State of the Union address, he pledged to help the economy prosper and create new jobs, in part, by spending additional government funds. In addition, he expressed a desire to return power to the states, a "New Federalism," saying:

> The time has now come in America to reverse the flow of power and resources from the States and communities to Washington, and start power and resources flowing back from Washington to the States and communities and, more important, to the people all across America.
>
> The time has come for a new partnership between the Federal Government and the States and localities—a partnership in which we entrust the States and localities with a larger share of the Nation's responsibilities, and in which we share our Federal revenues with them so that they can meet those responsibilities.

Nixon felt strongly that there were certain policies that the federal government could most effectively enact, such as universal health care and welfare reform. However, other concerns could be addressed locally if those government offices were given the money they needed. This message echoed through Nixon's later State of the Union addresses. He believed that more localized action would create an energy in the populace to come up with creative solutions to their problems. If people felt that government was responsive to their needs, then they would be more likely to participate in it.

Although Nixon's revenue-sharing proposal—the State and Local Assistance Act of 1972—was passed and became extremely popular, it was repealed in 1986. In fact, most of Nixon's New Federalism policies died following the Watergate scandal that ended his presidency.

See also: Block Grants; Federalist System; New Federalism; Richard Nixon's Campaign Speech to Visit All 50 States, in the Viewpoints Section.

FURTHER READING

Barron, Rachel Stiffler. *Richard Nixon: American Politician*. Greensboro, N.C.: Morgan Reynolds Publishing, 2004.

Black, Conrad. *Richard M. Nixon: A Life in Full*. New York: PublicAffairs Books, 2007.

Political Parties

Organizations that seek to gain and maintain power within a government, usually by participating in election campaigns. Political parties express an ideology or vision, offering voters a choice of policies and plans for the nation. Often, political parties have differing views on federalism. The first political parties in the United States formed in the 1790s, not long after the Constitution was ratified, though the Constitution does not include any provision for political parties.

The authors of the Constitution did not plan the new government of the United States with political parties in mind. In fact, many believed that political parties could lead to corruption and take away the freedom of the people to judge the issues in an election. Therefore, when George Washington (1789–1797) became the first president of the United States, he did not represent any political party. In addition, he chose Cabinet members who had various political philosophies instead of only those that supported his own views. Yet within a few years, the first political parties in the United States formed, each promoting very different views of how the new government should function. Today, political parties are an essential part of our **federal** system of government. They provide voters with alternative candidates and political philosophies. Parties are key to the nation's democratic processes.

FIRST POLITICAL PARTIES

The Federalist Party was one of the first two political parties to organize. Led by Vice President John Adams and Secretary of the Treasury Alexander Hamilton, the Federalists generally believed in a strong central government that could maintain order in the country.

Federalists Most Federalists were concentrated in New England, and many came from the elite upper classes. The Federalists were supported by merchants and manufacturers and had strong trade ties with **Great Britain**. Although George Washington did not consider himself a member of any political party, he was philosophically most like the Federalists.

Democratic-Republicans The second party to be established at this time was the Democratic-Republican Party, formed by then Secretary of State Thomas Jefferson and then Virginia congressman James Madison. The Democratic-Republicans were opposed to the Federalists and did not believe in a strong central government. They argued that the Constitution actually limited the powers of the federal government in order to give more power to the states and to the people. Jefferson and the Democratic-Republicans wanted the government to be made of up more than just the elite. They believed that all

M– R

adult white men should have the right to vote and hold political offices as long as they owned any amount of property, large or small.

The Democratic-Republican Party did not support close ties with Great Britain and often aligned itself politically with France, whose citizens had followed the American example in the late 1780s with their own revolution. The Democratic-Republicans believed that the United States should remain an agricultural country, unlike Great Britain, and therefore the party was most popular with farmers and Southerners.

Election of 1796 The presidential election of 1796 was the first in which voters could choose between two different political parties. The Federalists chose John Adams as their candidate, and the Democratic-Republicans chose Thomas Jefferson. Both parties set up the first election campaigns in order to gain support from voters.

John Adams (1797–1801) won the election, receiving the highest number of **electoral votes,** cast by the **Electoral College** that actually elects the president. However, because Thomas Jefferson won the second-highest number of electoral votes, he became vice president, which was how the electoral system worked at the time. Thus, the election of 1796 exposed a flaw in the Constitution because it did not take into account the rise of political parties.

Election of 1800 Four years later, in 1800, John Adams and Thomas Jefferson again ran against each other for president, but this time Jefferson (1801–1809) won. Aaron Burr became vice president. John Adams was in fact the only Federalist president of the United States.

Federalist Decline During the War of 1812 (1812–1814), in which the United States fought against Great Britain, many Federalists opposed the war because it kept them from trading with Great Britain. In 1814, some Federalists in the New England states wanted to **secede** from the United States and form their own country unless the American government ended the war with Britain.

After the war, many Americans considered the Federalists to be traitors for wanting to separate from the rest of the country. The Federalist Party fell apart by about 1820. This left the Democratic-Republican Party as the only political party in the United States until the middle of the 1820s.

Democratic-Republicans Split Although there was seemingly just one political party in the United States for a number of years, the Democratic-Republican Party was beginning to split into various **factions.** The split became increasingly evident by the end of James Monroe's presidency (1817–1825). Monroe, like George Washington, believed that the government should have no political divisions and, like Washington, he appointed leaders of various political philosophies to his Cabinet. He also took the position that Congress, not the president, was the best representative of the people, and therefore he weakened the role of the president and the executive branch of government. Monroe's presidency was the last one in which there was only one political party in the United States.

Thomas Jefferson wrote about the state of the Democratic-Republican Party in 1822: "An opinion prevails that there is no longer any distinction, that the republicans & Federalists are completely **amalgamated** but it is not so. . . . I trust . . . that the friends of the real constitution and union will prevail against consolidation, as they have done against monarchism."

Election of 1824 In the 1824 presidential election, four separate candidates from the Democratic-Republican Party ran for president. These were Secretary of the Treasury William H. Crawford, Secretary of State John Quincy Adams, House Speaker Henry Clay, and Tennessee senator Andrew Jackson. Jackson received the most popular votes, but not a majority, and the electoral votes were split four ways, with Jackson having the most. Because no candidate received a majority, the Constitution required that the election had to be decided by the **House of Representatives**. Speaker of the House Henry Clay decided to support John Quincy Adams. As a result, Adams (1825–1829) became president.

DEMOCRATS AND REPUBLICANS

Four years later, Andrew Jackson (1829–1837) won the presidency, and the faction of the Democratic-Republican Party that supported him eventually became what is now the Democratic Party. However, the name "Democratic Party" did not become official until 1844.

Andrew Jackson greatly expanded the role of the president in government, believing that the executive branch should carry more importance. As a result, a new political party formed in direct opposition to Jackson and the Democratic Party during the winter of 1833–1834. Led by John Quincy Adams and Henry Clay, the party was first called the National Republican Party and later became known as the Whig Party. The Whigs supported the power of Congress over the president and the executive branch.

A New Political Party In 1854, a new political party, the Republican Party, was founded by American **abolitionists** and others who opposed slavery. The Republican Party was also made up of members from the Whig Party, which had split over the issue of slavery and had greatly weakened. The new Republican Party stood not only against slavery but also for a strong central government. The Democrats in the South believed that Congress had no constitutional right to prohibit slavery, but the Republican Party believed that Congress had the right to bar it at least from the new western territories (many thought the Constitution protected slavery in the states where it already existed) and ought to do so. In 1860, Abraham Lincoln (1861–1865) became the first Republican candidate to win the presidency.

MODERN POLITICAL PARTIES

Following the presidency of Millard Fillmore (1850–1853), the last Whig

M– R

president, American presidents have belonged to one of two parties: the Republican or the Democratic Party. Each party has a distinct ideology and a different vision for the country in terms of governmental power, as well as economic and social issues. Although third-party candidates have run in many elections since then, they have never won a majority vote.

See also: Adams, John; Clay, Henry; Hamilton, Alexander; Jackson, Andrew; Jefferson, Thomas.

FURTHER READING

Adkins, Randall E., ed. *The Evolution of Political Parties, Campaigns and Elections: Landmark Documents from 1787–2008.* Washington, D.C.: CQ Press, 2008.

Aldrich, John H. ed. *Why Parties? The Origin and Transformation of Political Parties in America.* Chicago: University of Chicago Press, 1995.

Schulman, Bruce J., ed. *Student's Guide to Elections.* Washington, D.C.: CQ Press, 2008.

Popular Elections

See Direct Popular Election and Federalism.

Presidential Elections

See Electoral College System.

Reagan, Ronald (1911–2004)

The fortieth president of the United States, Ronald Reagan advocated a policy of New Federalism, planning to shift some governmental power back to the states.

A firm Democrat until the late 1940s, Reagan supported presidents Franklin D. Roosevelt (1933–1945) and Harry S. Truman (1945–1953). In the late 1940s, however, his political sympathies began to shift to the right as he became concerned about Communist influences in the country. He voted for Dwight Eisenhower (1953–1961) in 1952 and 1956 and Richard Nixon (1969–1974) in 1960. In 1962, Reagan officially registered as a Republican.

EARLY CAREER

After college, Ronald Reagan worked as a sportscaster for radio stations in Davenport and Des Moines, Iowa. During a trip to California in 1937 to cover the spring training sessions of the Chicago Cubs baseball team, an agent for the Warner Brothers movie studio persuaded Reagan to take a screen test. Reagan won the role of a small-town radio announcer, which started his movie career.

In 1942, Reagan entered the U.S. Army Air Corps; he was discharged in 1945 with the rank of captain. After World War II (1939–1945), he continued to act in movies but devoted an increasing amount of time to movie industry politics. In 1947, he was elected president of the Screen Actors Guild (SAG), a labor union representing Hollywood actors.

A NEW CAREER

In 1964, Reagan made a televised campaign speech on behalf of Republican presidential candidate Barry Goldwater. The speech established Reagan as a spokesman for the **conservative** wing of the Republican Party. This led California Republican leaders to ask him to run for governor in 1966. Reagan defeated **incumbent** Democrat Edmund G. Brown, who had beaten Richard Nixon four years before. Reagan was easily re-elected in 1970.

In 1976, Reagan sought the Republican presidential nomination against **incumbent** president Gerald R. Ford (1974–1977). Reagan came close to winning the nomination. Ford, however, received 1,187 delegate votes to Reagan's 1,070 delegate votes at the Republican National Convention. After Ford lost the election to Democrat Jimmy Carter (1977–1981), Reagan became the favorite to receive the Republican nomination in 1980.

During the next four years, Reagan campaigned for Republican candidates and raised money for his 1980 campaign. He won the 1980 Republican presidential nomination and went on to defeat incumbent Jimmy Carter in the general election, 489 **electoral votes** to 49.

A POPULAR PRESIDENT

During 1981, the Reagan administration focused on economic policy. The president pushed a large tax cut through Congress, along with increases in the defense budget and decreases in funding for many domestic programs. Reagan claimed that the tax cut would produce an economic boom. In turn, the economic upturn would lower unemployment while increasing tax revenues that would balance the **federal** budget. He also supported block grants to the states.

A severe **recession** that began in late 1981, however, increased unemployment to the highest level to that time since the **Great Depression** of the 1930s. In early 1983, the economy began to recover. Unlike economic recoveries during the 1970s, however, the expansion was not accompanied by high inflation. In the 1984 presidential election, with the economy prospering, Reagan overwhelmed his Democratic challenger, former vice president Walter F. Mondale, 525 to 13 in the **Electoral College.**

International Relations In foreign affairs, the first five years of Reagan's presidency were characterized by efforts to block Communist expansion and overturn pro-Communist governments in the developing world. With the rise of Mikhail Gorbachev as the leader of the Soviet Union in 1985, however, the president softened his anti-Communist language and began developing a working relationship with the Soviet leader. During his last three years in office, Reagan held five summits with Gorbachev and signed a treaty banning intermediate nuclear missiles in Europe.

However, Reagan's military buildup and tax cuts had worsened the nation's huge budget deficit. The national debt had risen from a little more than one trillion dollars when Reagan entered office in 1981 to more than two trillion dollars in 1986.

Later Years Reagan remained one of the most popular presidents of the late twentieth century. When Reagan's term ended in 1989, he returned to his home in Bel Air, California, and maintained a low public profile. In November 1994, Reagan announced in a handwritten note that he had been diagnosed with Alzheimer's

M–R

disease, which causes progressive mental and physical deterioration. He noted that he wanted his announcement to help raise awareness about the disease. Reagan died on June 5, 2004, at the age of 93.

See also: Block Grants; New Federalism.

FURTHER READING

Benson, Michael. *Ronald Reagan.* Minneapolis, Minn.: Lerner Publications, 2003.

Kengor, Paul. *The Crusader: Ronald Reagan and the Fall of Communism.* New York: Harper Perennial, 2007.

Reagan, Ronald. *The Reagan Diaries.* New York: HarperCollins, 2007.

Reapportionment and Redistricting

The redistribution among the states of the 435 seats in the **House of Representatives** to reflect shifts in population, and the redrawing within the states of congressional district boundaries for the House. These two procedures are among the most important and controversial processes in the U.S. political system. Together, reapportionment and redistricting help to determine whether Democrats or Republicans, liberals or conservatives will dominate the House. Thus, they have become an essential part of the nation's **federal** system of government.

FREQUENCY AND PROCESS
Reapportionment and redistricting occur every 10 years based on a census, a count of the nation's population. States in which populations grew quickly during the previous 10 years gain congressional seats, while those that lost population or grew much more slowly lose seats. The number of House members for the rest of the states remains the same.

The states that gain or lose seats usually must make extensive changes in their congressional maps. Even those states that keep the same number of representatives must make adjustments to take into account population shifts within their boundaries, in accordance with Supreme Court "one-person, one-vote" rulings.

In most states, the state legislatures are responsible for drafting and enacting the new congressional district map. Thus, the majority party in each state legislature is often in a position to draw a district map that enhances the fortunes of its **incumbents** and candidates at the expense of the opposing party.

THE FRAMERS' INTENTIONS
What did the Framers of the Constitution have in mind about who would be represented in the House of Representatives and how? The Constitution declares only that each state is to be allotted a certain number of representatives. It does not state specifically that congressional districts must be equal or nearly equal in population. Nor does it require that a state create districts at all. However, it seems clear that the first clause of Article I, Section 2, of the Constitution, providing that House members should be chosen "by the People of the several States," indicates that House of Representatives was to represent people rather than states. The

The taking of the Census every 10 years is a key element of the nation's federal system. The information from the Census allows Congress to redistribute the 435 seats in the House of Representatives to help ensure equal representation for all citizens.

third clause of Article I, Section 2, provided that congressional apportionment among the states must be according to population.

REAPPORTIONMENT: THE NUMBER OF SEATS IN THE HOUSE OF REPRESENTATIVES

The Constitution made the first apportionment, which was to remain in effect until the first Census was taken. No reliable figures on the population were available at the time. The Constitution's apportionment yielded a 65-member House. The seats were allotted among the 13 states as follows: New Hampshire, 3; Massachusetts, 8; Rhode Island and Providence Plantations, 1; Connecticut, 5; New York, 6; New Jersey, 4; Pennsylvania, 8; Delaware, 1; Maryland, 6; Virginia, 10; North Carolina, 5; South Carolina, 5; and Georgia, 3. This apportionment remained in effect during the First and Second Congresses (1789–1793).

Apportionment by Congress Congress enacted apportionment legislation after the first Census was taken

A Seat in the House

In the first Congress (1789–1791), each member of the House of Representatives represented about 30,000 people. Because the population of each state was not known, the Constitution provided the number of representatives for each of the 13 states. The Constitution also provided for a census, or a count of the population of each state, to take place every 10 years. The first Census took place in 1790 and showed that the young United States had a population of 3,929,326, of which 697,681 were enslaved.

Throughout the years, the number of members in the House increased as the population of the nation grew, and in 1911, Congress fixed the number at 435. In addition, Congress has used various methods to determine the number of represen-

tatives from each state, trying to be as fair as possible. Indeed, reapportionment of House seats is one of the most contentious actions of Congress.

The 22nd Census, taken in 2000, determined that the population of the United States was 281,421,906. Using the data provided by the Census, Congress reapportioned the 435 seats of the House, increasing the number of seats for states with growing populations, while decreasing the number of seats for those states with declining populations. Thus, each member of the House represents a population of about 647,000—a vast increase since 1789. A census will be conducted in 2010, and Congress will again reapportion the 435 seats of the House, unless it decides to increase the number of members in the House.

in 1790. The first apportionment bill was sent to President George Washington (1789–1797) in March 1792. The bill had included the constitutional minimum of 30,000 as the size of each district. The population of each state, however, was not a simple multiple of 30,000; significant fractions were left over. For example, Vermont was found to be entitled to 2.85 representatives, New Jersey to 5.98, and Virginia to 21.02.

The president sent the bill back to Congress without his signature. This was the first presidential **veto.** Washington's veto was based on the belief that eight states would receive more than one representative for each 30,000 people under this plan.

A motion to override the veto was unsuccessful. A new bill, meeting the president's objections, passed in April 1792. It provided for a ratio of one member for every 33,000 inhabitants and fixed the exact number of representatives to which each state was entitled. The total membership of the House was to be 105. In dividing the population of the various states by 33,000, all remainders were to be disregarded. Thomas Jefferson (1801–1809) devised this solution, known as the method of rejected fractions.

UNHAPPINESS WITH JEFFERSON'S METHOD

Dissatisfaction with inequalities produced by the method of rejected fractions grew. Representative Daniel Webster urged adoption of a method that would assign an additional representative to each state with a large fraction.

Following the 1840 Census, Congress adopted a reapportionment method similar to that advocated by Webster. The method fixed a ratio of one representative for every 70,680 people. This figure was reached by deciding on a fixed size of the House in advance (223), dividing that figure into the total national "representative population," and using the result (70,680) as the fixed ratio. The population of each state was then divided by this ratio to find the number of its representatives, and the states were assigned an additional representative for each fraction more than one-half. Under this method, the actual size of the House dropped.

The modified reapportionment formula adopted by Congress in 1842 was more satisfactory than the previous method, but another change was made following the Census of 1850. Proposed by Ohio representative Samuel F. Vinton, the new system became known as the Vinton method.

VINTON FORMULA

Under the Vinton formula, Congress first fixed the size of the House and then distributed the seats. The total qualifying population of the country was divided by the desired number of representatives, and the resulting number became the ratio of population to each representative. The population of each state was divided by this ratio, and each state received the number of representatives equal to

the whole number in the quotient for that state. Then, to reach the required size of the House, additional representatives were assigned based on the remaining fractions, beginning with the state having the largest fraction.

Those who favored the Vinton method pointed out that it had the advantage of fixing the size of the House in advance and taking into account at least the largest fractions. The concern of the House turned from the ideal size of a congressional district to the ideal size of the House itself.

Six reapportionments were carried out using the Vinton method—1850, 1860, 1870, 1880, 1890, and 1900. Other reapportionment acts increased the size of the House—241 members in 1862; 283 in 1872; 325 in 1882; 356 in 1892; and 386 in 1902.

MAXIMUM MEMBERSHIP OF HOUSE

In 1911, the membership of the House was fixed at 433 representatives. Provision was made for the addition of one representative each from Arizona and New Mexico, which were expected to become states in the near future. Thus, the size of the House reached 435, where it has remained with the exception of a brief period, 1959–1963, when the admission of Alaska and Hawaii raised the total temporarily to 437.

Limiting the size of the House was recognition that the body soon would expand to an unmanageable size if Congress continued the practice of adding new seats every 10 years to

M–R

match population gains without depriving any state of its existing representation. Agreement on a fixed number made the task of reapportionment even more difficult because the population not only increased but also became much more mobile.

A new calculation method was adopted for the reapportionment following the 1910 Census. This new system established a priority list that assigned seats progressively, beginning with the first seat above the constitutional minimum of at least one seat for each state. When there were 48 states, this method was used to assign the 49th member, the 50th member, and so on, until the agreed upon size of the House was reached. The method was called major fractions and was used after the Censuses of 1910, 1930, and 1940. There was no reapportionment after the 1920 Census.

The results of the 1920 Census were announced in December, just after the short session of the Sixty-sixth Congress convened. The 1920 Census showed that for the first time in history most Americans were urban, or city, residents. During the early 1920s, Congress considered several reapportionment bills, but these were blocked in committees by rural representatives who believed that rural residents were undercounted.

METHOD OF EQUAL PROPORTIONS

Congress adopted a new "equal proportions" method to be used in reapportionment calculations after the 1950 and subsequent Censuses. The method of equal proportions involves complicated mathematical calculations. It is designed to make the proportional difference in the average district size in any two states as small as possible. After the 2000 reapportionment, for example, average population per district increased to 647,000. Montana's single district was the most populous with 902,195 people. Wyoming's single district was the least populous with 493,782 residents.

REDISTRICTING: DRAWING THE LINES

Although the Constitution contained provisions for the apportionment of U.S. House seats among the states, it was silent about how the members should be elected. From the beginning, most states divided their territory into geographic districts, permitting only one member of Congress to be elected from each district.

Some states allowed would-be House members to run at large, with voters able to cast as many votes as there were seats to be filled. Still other states created what were known as multimember districts, in which a single geographic unit would elect two or more members of the House. At various times, some states used combinations of these methods. For example, a state might elect 10 representatives from 10 individual districts and 2 at large.

Those states that used congressional districts quickly developed what came to be known as the **gerrymander.** The term refers to the practice of drawing district lines so as to maximize the advantage of a political party or interest group. The name originated from a salamander-shaped congressional district created by the Massachusetts legislature in 1812 when Elbridge Gerry was governor.

Constant efforts were made during the early 1800s to lay down national rules, by means of a constitutional amendment, for congressional districting. In Congress, Senator Mahlon Dickerson proposed such an amendment regularly almost every year from 1817 to 1826. It was adopted by the **Senate** three times, in 1819, 1820, and 1822, but each time it failed to reach a vote in the House. Although the constitutional amendment was unsuccessful, a law passed in 1842 required single-member congressional districts. That law required representatives to be

> ... elected by districts composed of contiguous [connected] territory equal in number to the representatives to which said state may be entitled, no one district electing more than one Representative.

Several unsuccessful attempts were made to enforce redistricting provisions. Despite the districting requirements enacted in 1842, New Hampshire, Georgia, Mississippi, and Missouri elected their representatives at large that autumn. However, by 1848 all four states had changed to electing their representatives by districts.

Court Action on Redistricting After the deadlock over reapportionment in the 1920s, those who were unhappy over the inaction of Congress and the state legislatures began taking their cases to court. At first, the protesters had no luck. As the population inequality grew in both federal and state legislative districts, and the Supreme Court began to show a tendency to intervene, the objectors were more successful.

Finally, in a series of decisions beginning in 1962 with *Baker v. Carr,* the Court exerted great influence over the redistricting process, ordering that congressional districts as well as state and local legislative districts be drawn so that their populations would be as equal as possible.

Congress and Redistricting Congress considered several proposals in the post–World War II (1939–1945) period to enact new legislation on redistricting. Only one of these efforts was successful—enactment of a measure barring at-large elections in states with more than one House seat. Exceptions were made for New Mexico and Hawaii, which had a tradition of electing their representatives at large. Both states, however, soon passed districting laws, New Mexico for the 1968 elections and Hawaii for 1970.

Bills to increase the size of the House to prevent states from losing seats as a result of population shifts have been introduced after most recent Censuses. Congress, however, has given little consideration to any of them.

See also: Census; Constitutional Convention.

Redistricting and Reapportionment, 1910 and 2000

Membership in the U.S. House of Representatives, after 1910 Census

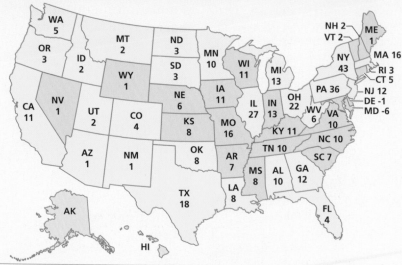

WA 5
OR 3
ID 2
MT 2
ND 3
SD 3
MN 10
WI 11
MI 13
NH 2
VT 2
ME 1
NY 43
MA 16
RI 3
CT 5
PA 36
NJ 12
DE -1
MD -6
CA 11
NV 1
UT 2
CO 4
WY 1
NE 6
IA 11
IL 27
IN 13
OH 22
WV 6
VA 10
KY 11
KS 8
MO 16
NC 10
AZ 1
NM 1
OK 8
AR 7
TN 10
SC 7
MS 8
AL 10
GA 12
TX 18
LA 8
FL 4
AK
HI

Membership in the U.S. House of Representatives, after 2000 Census

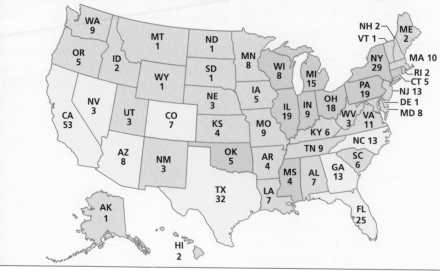

WA 9
OR 5
ID 2
MT 1
ND 1
MN 8
WI 8
MI 15
NH 2
VT 1
ME 2
NY 29
MA 10
RI 2
CT 5
PA 19
NJ 13
DE 1
MD 8
CA 53
NV 3
UT 3
CO 7
WY 1
NE 3
IA 5
IL 19
IN 9
OH 18
WV 3
VA 11
KY 6
KS 4
MO 9
NC 13
AZ 8
NM 3
OK 5
AR 4
TN 9
SC 6
MS 4
AL 7
GA 13
TX 32
LA 7
FL 25
AK 1
HI 2

| Representation increased since last census | Representation decreased since last census | Representation stayed the same | Non-voting territories |

© Infobase Publishing

Reapportionment, or redistribution, of the membership of the House of Representatives ensures that citizens are fairly represented. Whereas population shifts to the South and West in about 100 years have caused an increase in the number of representatives from states in those regions, states in the North and Midwest have lost representatives.

FURTHER READING

Koestler-Grack, Rachel A. *The House of Representatives.* New York: Chelsea House, 2007.

Redistricting

See Reapportionment and Redistricting.

S–T

Seventeenth Amendment (1913)

A change added to the original U.S. Constitution of 1789 that modified the balance of the **federalist** system, moving powers away from state **legislatures** and giving them to the voters. The **amendment** required the direct election of senators by the people of a state rather than appointment by the state legislature. The Seventeenth Amendment also gives power to the governor of each state to appoint a senator, if an opening occurs, until an election can take place.

CONSTITUTIONAL FRAMEWORK

The U.S. Constitution established the legislative branch of the government, which consisted of two houses, the **House of Representatives** and the **Senate**. Each member of the House of Representatives represents a district in his or her state. The number of representatives in each state is dependent upon that state's population, meaning that states with large populations have more representatives than states with small populations. Each state has two senators, regardless of that state's population.

Because the Framers of the Constitution were cautious about **democracy** in government and wanted a balance within the legislative branch, they decided that, while members of the House of Representatives could be directly elected by the people of their states, the members of the Senate should be elected by state legislatures. The Framers felt that because senators would not have to worry about reelection and trying to win the popular vote, they could better focus on the nation's issues.

MOVE TO DIRECT ELECTION

Republican senators Robert La Follette of Wisconsin and George Norris of Nebraska strongly supported direct election of senators by the people. Every year, from 1893 to 1902, a constitutional amendment to elect senators by popular vote was proposed in Congress, but most members of the Senate rejected it.

Before **ratification** of the Seventeenth Amendment, however, many states had changed their own laws so that voters had more influence over the selection of senators. Voters participating in **primary elections** designated their preference for one of the parties' candidates for a senatorial seat. Usually, the state legislatures supported the people's preference. By 1912, 29 states were nominating senators on some type of popular basis. In 1911, Senator Joseph Bristow from Kansas proposed an

S–T

amendment to the Constitution. Those senators who had been chosen only by their respective state legislatures fought against the bill. Ultimately, however, the majority of the Senate approved the bill because of the vote of those senators who had been chosen by the state legislatures with the guidance of the preference system.

After the Senate passed the bill, the House passed it in summer 1912. Finally, it was sent to the states for ratification. Connecticut became the 36th state to ratify the Seventeenth Amendment in April 1913, giving the amendment the required three-fourths majority necessary to be added to the Constitution. The following year all elections for senator were held by popular vote.

See also: Constitutional Convention; Direct Popular Election and Federalism.

Shared Powers

Those governmental powers that are held at the same time by both the national government and the state governments, an essential part of a **federal** system of government. Under the U.S. Constitution, the states may share with the national government any power that is not solely granted to the federal government. The power cannot be plainly denied to the states.

The national and state governments share the power to set up courts, make and enforce laws, and spend money for the general welfare. A state may regulate intrastate **commerce,** or commerce within its boundaries. The national government, however, has the power to regulate interstate commerce, or commerce among the states. The shared powers among the different levels of government are a key characteristic of the nation's federal system.

See also: Articles of Confederation; Constitutional Convention; Federalist System.

FURTHER READING
Genovese, Michael A., and Lori Cox Han. *Encyclopedia of American Government and Civics.* New York: Facts On File, 2008.

Shays's Rebellion (1786–1787)

An armed uprising in western Massachusetts led by Daniel Shays, a farmer who had served as a captain in the American Revolution (1775–1783). Because the national government was unable to respond to the uprising, Shays's Rebellion is considered an important factor leading up to the Constitutional Convention of 1787, which set out to write a new constitution for the United States. This new constitution would create a **federal** system of government.

By the end of the American Revolution, the United States was suffering from an economic depression and enormous debt. Soldiers of the Continental Army were sent home from the war with little or no pay because, under the Articles of Confederation, Congress had no power to raise money to pay them. Each state was responsible for its own war debt. In Massachusetts, the state legislature had voted to pay off their debt by heavily taxing land, which greatly affected the farmers of western Massachusetts. By 1786, nearly 2,000 farmers in western Massachusetts were threatened with **foreclosure** of their property or imprisonment for failure to repay debts.

THE FARMERS REACT

That year, farmers in various towns of western Massachusetts, many of whom had been soldiers in the Continental Army, met to discuss their increasingly desperate situation. At first, the farmers sent petitions to the state government, asking that taxes be reduced and that their farms not be seized for lack of payment. When the government did not respond to their requests, the farmers decided to take further action.

On August 29, 1786, a group of men led by Daniel Shays occupied the courthouse in Northampton, making it impossible for the court to imprison debtors or seize their property. These men called themselves the

---

HISTORY MAKERS
Daniel Shays (c. 1747–1825)

Daniel Shays was born in Hopkinton, Massachusetts, around 1747. Not much is known about his early life, but it is likely that he hired himself out to work on farms.

Around 1774, Shays moved west to Shutesbury, where he joined a militia. By 1777, Shays had become Captain in the Fifth Massachusetts Regiment of the Continental Army. During the American Revolution (1775–1783), Shays fought in the famous battles of Bunker Hill, Ticonderoga, Saratoga, and Stony Point.

Shays resigned from the army in 1780 and settled in Pelham, Massachusetts. By 1786, he had become a leader of a group of farmers in western Massachusetts who protested the heavy taxes imposed by the state government. Shays and his men, who called themselves the Regulators, surrounded town courts to prevent them from conducting business, so that they could not seize property or put farmers in prison for unpaid debt. This uprising later became known as Shays's Rebellion.

In January 1787, Shays and his men were fired upon by a government militia hired specifically to stop the rebels. The Regulators were eventually forced to surrender. Shays then fled to Vermont. He was condemned to death on charge of treason, but eventually he and other rebels were pardoned by Massachusetts governor John Hancock.

Shays eventually moved to upstate New York and continued to farm. In his old age, he was finally granted a monthly pension by the federal government for his service in the American Revolution. Daniel Shays died in 1825 at the age of 78.

S–T

"Regulators." They wore their old Continental Army uniforms with a sprig of hemlock in their hats to identify themselves. In late September of that year, Daniel Shays again led a group of more than 1,000 men to occupy the Springfield courthouse to prevent the Supreme Judicial Court from doing business. For the next few months, the Regulators, led by Shays and others, marched through various towns in western Massachusetts, armed with clubs and muskets, and surrounded the courthouses to keep them closed.

FIGHTING TYRANNY

Daniel Shays and the Regulators insisted that they were not leading a rebellion but rather continuing the fight against tyranny as the colonists had done in 1776. Yet many of the wealthy merchants and legislators in Boston viewed things differently. They panicked and feared that society as they knew it was falling apart. In response, Congress authorized the raising of troops to fight the rebels, but the national government had no power to raise money for an army. Finally, Massachusetts governor James Bowdoin and some Boston merchants used their own money to hire a **militia** of more than 4,000 men to stop the revolt.

In January 1787, Daniel Shays and about 1,500 Regulators marched to the government **arsenal** in Springfield to supply their men with more arms. When Shays's group arrived, they were met by the government militia from Boston. The militia fired cannons into the group, killing 4 men and wounding 20. The Regulators retreated and were eventually forced to surrender. Shays and other rebels fled to Vermont, which was not yet part of the Union.

A Harsh Sentence In April, the Supreme Judicial Court sentenced 14 of the rebellion's leaders, including Shays, to death for treason. However, in the election that June, conservative Governor James Bowdoin was defeated by John Hancock, who had previously been governor of Massachusetts as well as president of the Continental Congress. Hancock and the new administration soon enacted debt relief for the farmers of western Massachusetts and were much more lenient toward the former rebels, eventually pardoning them.

IMPORTANCE OF THE REBELLION

Shays's Rebellion had a huge impact on many Americans who feared that similar rebellions could spread across all 13 states. This, in addition to the economic crisis the country was facing, only underscored the fact that the Articles of Confederation amounted to a weak form of government, unable to solve basic economic and social problems. This ultimately helped persuade the states to send **delegates** to the Constitutional Convention in Philadelphia in May 1787 to create a stronger central government.

At the Constitutional Convention, George Washington, who had reentered public life for just the purpose of the convention, referred to Shays's Rebellion when he declared that "there could be no stronger evidence of the want of energy in our governments than these disorders."

Federalist James Madison urged the delegates to support his Virginia Plan, with its strong central government, insisting that, "The rebellion in Massachusetts is a warning, gentlemen." Madison's Virginia Plan formed the basis for the U.S. Constitution, ratified in 1788.

See also: Constitutional Convention; Jefferson, Thomas; Washington, George.

FURTHER READING

Burgan, Michael. *Shays' Rebellion.* Minneapolis, Minn.: Compass Point Books, 2008.

Richards, Leonard L. *Shays's Rebellion: The American Revolution's Final Battle.* Philadelphia: University of Pennsylvania Press, 2002.

Sherman, Roger

See Connecticut Compromise.

States' Rights

The idea that the individual states of the United States have certain rights and powers in relation to the **federal** government. There has been much debate in American history regarding how much power the U.S. Constitution grants the federal government and what the individual states' rights are.

States' rights are supported by the Tenth Amendment, which is a part of the Bill of Rights, or the first 10 amendments to the Constitution. The Tenth Amendment declares that all powers not specifically delegated to the federal government are powers reserved for the states. States rights' supporters insist on a strict, or literal, interpretation of this amendment.

SUPREMACY CLAUSE

The Articles of Confederation (1781–1788), the first written plan of government for the United States, gave the central government very little authority to overrule state actions. The Constitution, which was ratified in 1788, strengthened the central government and sought a balance between the state and federal governments. In the event of any conflict between state and federal law, the Supremacy Clause of Article VI of the Constitution resolves the conflict in favor of the federal government. It declares federal law the "supreme law of the land." However, the Supremacy Clause only applies if the federal government is acting within the boundaries of its constitutionally authorized powers.

During the writing of the Constitution, those who favored states' rights over a stronger central government feared there might be power struggles between the federal government and the state governments if the Constitution did not clearly spell out that powers not granted to the federal government would be powers granted to the states. The Tenth Amendment was written to affirm explicitly what had only been implied in the Constitution. It also reassured the states that state and local governments could continue to exercise their power and be accountable to the people in their communities.

ONGOING CONFLICT

Until the Civil War, the states' rights debate usually involved the question of state **sovereignty**, or the exclusive right to have control over an area of governance. Because the states were sovereign under the Articles of Confederation, some state leaders claimed that the states remained sovereign under the Constitution. This would have given them the power to **secede** from the Union or to **nullify,** or cancel, acts of Congress. During the late 1700s and early 1800s, various states threatened secession over federal laws or actions that they did not approve of, but it was not until 1861 that South Carolina became the first state to secede from the Union.

Virginia and Kentucky Resolutions In 1798, the members of the Federalist Party in Congress passed the Alien and Sedition Acts, four laws whose purpose was to strengthen the federal government's powers. However, these were seen by many as a threat to individual rights. Under the Alien Act, the president could expel any alien, or noncitizen, believed to be dangerous to the nation's security. Under the Sedition Act, it became illegal to "write, print, utter, or publish" anything critical of the president or Congress. About 20 newspaper editors were forced to shut down their papers, arrested, and fined or sentenced to 18 months in prison under this law.

Vice President Thomas Jefferson and Virginia representative James Madison, supporters of states' rights, responded to the Alien and Sedition Acts by anonymously writing the Kentucky and Virginia Resolutions, (also known as the Kentucky and Virginia Resolves) which declared that the federal government had no right to exercise powers not specifically

delegated to it. The Kentucky and Virginia Resolutions rejected the Alien and Sedition Acts as unconstitutional and called upon other states to reject them. Ultimately, the Alien and Sedition Acts expired in 1800 and 1801 and were not renewed.

War of 1812 Another states' rights dispute occurred during the War of 1812 (1812–1814), which was fought between the United States and **Great Britain**. In 1814, some Federalists in New England wanted to secede from the United States and form their own country unless the American government ended the war. After the United States emerged victorious in the war, the Federalists were viewed by many as traitors, and this ultimately led to the collapse of the Federalist Party.

Slavery Over the following decades, the issue of slavery became the most important and controversial states' rights issue, and it ultimately divided the nation. Supporters of slavery argued that slavery was a local issue and that states had the right to protect slave property. In contrast, opponents of slavery argued that slavery was a national issue and that Congress had the right to prohibit its spread into the Western territories.

Civil Rights Movement During the civil rights movement of the 1950s and 1960s, state laws that supported racial **segregation** of African Americans were challenged, though many states argued that states' rights prohibited the federal government from interfering with state laws. Though the Fifteenth Amendment granted African American males the right to vote in 1870, this law was strongly resisted in the South. By the 1890s, many Southern states had amended their constitutions and enacted a series of laws to prevent African Americans from voting. Congress finally passed the Voting Rights Act of 1965 that guaranteed African Americans the rights that had been granted to them by the Fifteenth Amendment.

In recent times, states' rights supporters continue to oppose the concentration of power in the national government and argue that the federal government should not be involved in what they consider states' issues, such as education and welfare. However, the powers of the federal government have generally expanded throughout the course of American history.

See also: Tenth Amendment; Voting Rights Act (1965).

FURTHER READING

Drake, Frederick D., and Lynn R. Nelson, eds. *States' Rights and American Federalism: A Documentary History*. Westport, Conn.: Greenwood Press, 1999.

Strict Constructionist

A person who believes that the U.S. Constitution should be interpreted strictly, or literally. Strict constructionists maintain that when interpreting the Constitution, only its specific wording and the original intentions of its authors should be considered. This contrasts with loose constructionists, who believe that the Constitution should be interpreted broadly and therefore adapted to the needs of a changing society.

After the Constitution was ratified in 1788, many anti-Federalists, or those who favored states' rights over a strong central government, including Thomas Jefferson and James Madison, took a strict constructionist position. They believed that a strict interpretation of the Constitution would ensure that most of the governmental power would remain with the states and not be taken over by the central government through broad interpretations of the national government's powers.

One of the first disputes between strict constructionists and loose constructionists arose in 1791, when Alexander Hamilton, the first secretary of the Treasury of the United States, proposed establishing the First Bank of the United States, modeled after the Bank of England. Faced with an enormous debt after the American Revolution (1775–1783), Hamilton's bank bill was to establish a national bank that would collect taxes, hold government money, and make loans to the government and borrowers. It would also create a standard form of currency because, at the time, each state had its own currency. The First Bank was to be set up as a business like any other business in the country. President George Washington (1789–1797), hesitant about signing this bill into law, asked for a written opinion from all his Cabinet members about the establishment of a national bank.

JEFFERSON'S VIEW

Taking the strict constructionist position, then Secretary of State Thomas Jefferson insisted that a national bank was unconstitutional because the

Constitution did not specifically give Congress the power to create a bank. Jefferson wrote: "To take a single step beyond the boundaries thus specially drawn around the powers of Congress, is to take possession of a boundless field of power, no longer susceptible of any definition. . . . The incorporation of a bank, and the powers assumed by this bill, have not, in my opinion, been delegated to the United States, by the Constitution."

HAMILTON'S VIEW

Alexander Hamilton, however, took the loose constructionist position. He pointed out that because of the specific wording of the Constitution, "there will be cases clearly within the power of the national government; others, clearly without its powers; and a third class, which will leave room for controversy and difference of opinion, and concerning which a reasonable latitude of judgment must be allowed." Therefore, because this issue fell into this last category, Hamilton argued that Congress did have the power to create a bank because the Constitution grants the **federal** government authority to do anything "necessary and proper" to carry out its constitutional functions. George Washington, persuaded by Hamilton's argument, signed the bank bill into law in April 1791.

THE ISSUE TODAY

Today, debate in the United States continues concerning how the Supreme Court should interpret the Constitution. Strict constructionists firmly believe that the justices must always interpret the Constitution as the authors intended. On the other hand, loose constructionists note that this approach does not always produce a balanced result. They point out that the Constitution is a "living document" that must be adapted to contemporary circumstances which the nation's **Founders** could not have anticipated. The ongoing debate reflects the differing views on the balance of power within a federal system.

See also: Hamilton, Alexander; Loose Constructionist; Jefferson, Thomas; States' Rights.

FURTHER READING

Kluge, Dave. *The People's Guide to the United States Constitution.* Glendale, Calif.: Action Publishing, 2007.

Schultz, David. *Encyclopedia of the U.S. Constitution.* New York: Facts On File, 2009.

Supreme Court and Federalism

See *McCulloch v. Maryland* (1819); *Gibbons v. Ogden* (1824).

Tenth Amendment (1791)

A change added to the original U.S. Constitution stating that any powers that are not granted to the national government by the Constitution are powers granted to the states. The Tenth Amendment supports the system of federalism in the United States, a system in which the power to govern is shared between a strong central government and smaller state governments.

The Tenth Amendment is part of the Bill of Rights, or the first 10 amendments to the Constitution.

Because the Constitution established a strong central government, many anti-Federalists at the Constitutional Convention insisted that a Bill of Rights be added to the Constitution to ensure that individual rights were protected. After the passage of the Constitution, the Bill of Rights was introduced to the first U.S. Congress in 1789. The 10 amendments together were added to the Constitution in 1791, after they had been **ratified** by three-fourths of the states.

FEDERALIST VIEW

During the time of debate over the Bill of Rights, many Federalists argued that an amendment granting power to the states was unnecessary because the powers of the **federal** government were carefully spelled out in the original Constitution.

Because the Constitution does not give Congress, the president, or the federal justice system the power to regulate local issues, the Federalists felt that it was clear which powers would be left to the states.

ANTI-FEDERALIST VIEW

Yet, anti-Federalists such as Thomas Jefferson feared there could be power struggles between the federal government and state governments if the Constitution did not clearly spell out that powers not granted to the federal government would be powers granted to the states. According to Jefferson, "The States should be left to do whatever acts they can do as well as the General Government."

The Tenth Amendment was written to spell out explicitly what had only been implied in the Constitution. It also reassured the states that

S–
T

Power to the States

The Tenth Amendment states that any powers that are not granted to the national government by the Constitution are powers granted to the states. It is part of the Bill of Rights, or the first 10 amendments to the Constitution.

Since the Civil War, the issue of states' rights has been challenged numerous times, requiring the Supreme Court to decide how to interpret the Tenth Amendment in each case. It is likely that the balance of power between the state and federal governments will continue to be challenged for years to come.

The powers not delegated to the United States by the Constitution, nor prohibited by it to the States, are reserved to the States respectively, or to the people.

state and local governments could continue to exercise their power and be accountable to the people in their communities.

Thomas Jefferson stated that the Tenth Amendment was "the foundation of the Constitution" and that "to take a single step beyond the boundaries thus specifically drawn around the powers of Congress is to take possession of a boundless field of power, no longer susceptible of any definition."

See also: Constitutional Convention; States' Rights.

FURTHER READING

Hudson, David L., Jr. *The Bill of Rights: The First Ten Amendments of the Constitution.* Berkeley Heights, N.J.: Enslow Publishers, 2002.

Patrick, John J. *The Bill of Rights: A History in Documents.* New York: Oxford University Press, 2003.

Smith, Rick. *Ninth and Tenth Amendments: The Right to More Rights.* Edina, Minn.: ABDO and Daughters, 2007.

V–W

Virginia and Kentucky Resolutions

Documents written anonymously by James Madison and Thomas Jefferson in response to the Alien and Sedition Acts, which had been passed by the Federalist-controlled Congress in 1798. These **resolutions** (sometimes called "resolves") declared that the Union had been created by an agreement among the states. Thus, the **federal** government had been created by the states and the states had the right to determine when the national government exceeded its authority.

THE ALIEN AND SEDITION ACTS

During the late 1790s, the United States and France fought an undeclared war on the high seas. The Federalist Party, which controlled the presidency and Congress at the time, was concerned about the criticism from Republican editors and writers, some of whom were refugees from France. These writers and editors heaped abuse upon governmental officials for what they considered an anti-French foreign policy. Federalists looked upon these writers as pro-French and were fearful of their radical views. The Federalists decided that the national interest required the suppression of criticism in a period of crisis.

In summer 1798, the Federalist-dominated Congress passed a series of acts to deal with the Republican opposition that they believed to be subversive. These acts, called the Alien and Sedition Acts, included the Naturalization Act, the Alien Act, the Alien Enemies Act, and the Sedition Act.

The Naturalization Act raised the period of living in the United States before securing American citizenship from 5 to 14 years. The Alien Act gave the president the power to order the deportation of any **alien** considered dangerous to the national welfare. The Alien Enemies Act empowered the president, in times of war, to either deport or imprison aliens of an enemy nation.

The harshest of the acts, however, was the Sedition Act, which was aimed directly at Republican leaders. Persons found guilty of "combining and conspiring to oppose the execution of the laws, or publishing false, scandalous, or malicious writings against the president, Congress, or government of the United States" might be imprisoned and fined. Before the end of John Adams's

History Speaks

The Kentucky Resolution

The Virginia and Kentucky Resolutions (or Resolves), written in response to the Federalist-supported Alien and Sedition Acts, were among the first documents detailing the theory of states' rights. In this excerpt from the Kentucky Resolution, writer Thomas Jefferson clearly notes that the Constitution is an agreement made by the individual states and that laws of the federal government can be judged, or approved, by the states.

Resolved, that the several States compromising the United States of America, are not united on the principle of unlimited submission to their general government; but that by a compact under the style and title of a Constitution for the United States and of amendments thereto, they constituted a general government for special purposes, delegated to that government certain definite powers, reserving each State to itself, the residuary mass of right of self government [most of the powers of self government]; and that whensoever the general government assumes undelegated powers, its acts are unauthoratative, void, and of no force. That to this compact [the Constitution] each States acceded as a State, and is an integral party, the co-States forming, as to itself, the other party: That the government created by this compact was not made the exclusive or final judge of the extent of the powers delegated to itself; since that have made its discretion, and not the Constitution, the measure of its powers; but that as in all other cases of compact among parties having no common Judge, *each party has an equal right to judge for itself, as well as infractions as of the mode and measure of redress.*

V–W

presidency (1797–1801), several Republican editors had been fined or imprisoned for violating the act.

REPUBLICAN RESPONSE TO THE ACTS

Clearly, the Alien and Sedition Acts violated the principles of freedom of speech and freedom of the press guaranteed by the Bill of Rights. Republicans, convinced that the acts were aimed directly at them, made heroes of those convicted and actively opposed the acts. They also denounced the Federalists. The Republicans believed that the acts were not only a threat to the Bill of Rights but also an unlawful attempt to extend the power of the federal government.

The Virginia and Kentucky Resolutions (also known as the Virginia and Kentucky Resolves) forcefully expressed the Republican view. James Madison drew up resolutions that were passed by the Virginia legislature, and Thomas Jefferson wrote similar resolutions that were passed in Kentucky.

Declaring that the states had created the Union, the resolutions claimed that the federal government was intended to serve the states on matters of common concern, such as national defense. The federal government, the resolutions continued, could not be the final judge of its own powers. Thus, the states had to have the power to decide when the federal government abused its power.

The arguments put forth in the Virginia and Kentucky Resolutions would later be used to support states' rights issues, especially in regard to the question of slavery. With the election of Thomas Jefferson (1801–1809) as president in 1800, the potential crisis over the Virginia and Kentucky Resolutions passed. Soon after taking office in 1801, Jefferson let the acts expire.

See also: Adams, John; Jefferson, Thomas; States' Rights.

FURTHER READING

Behrman, Carol H. *Thomas Jefferson.* Minneapolis, Minn.: Lerner Publications, 2004.

Roberts, Jeremy. *James Madison.* Minneapolis, Minn.: Lerner Publications, 2004.

Watkins, William. *Reclaiming the American Revolution: The Kentucky and Virginia Resolutions and Their Legacy.* New York: Palgrave Macmillan, 2008.

Voter Registration

The method usually used to identify voters who are qualified to participate in an election, a right that the **federal** government works to protect. Voters register by submitting proof to authorized officials that they have met the prescribed qualifications.

A STATE DECISION

Although many of the original state constitutions that were drafted between 1776 and 1780 included property qualifications for voting, the U.S. Constitution does not include any restrictions. Qualifications for voting were left up to the individual states. Since that time, however, the federal government has intervened to guarantee that all state requirements are reasonable and do not deny eligible voters the right to register or cast ballots.

The issue of voting rights in the United States has been a long struggle for various groups over the course of American history. Though each state determines which citizens have the right to vote in that state, over time, constitutional amendments and other federal laws have been passed to impose national standards on state voting laws.

Before the 1820s, most states imposed property restrictions on voting, meaning that only white men with property could vote. This changed, partly because of the influence of President Andrew Jackson (1829–1837), and by 1830, all white male adult citizens could vote. Jackson, considered a "man of the people," believed that even the common man had the right to make his voice heard in American politics.

INCREASING VOTING RIGHTS

However, securing the right to vote for African Americans and women was a much longer struggle. Before the Civil War (1861–1865), a few Northern states allowed free black men to vote. Restrictive state laws and slavery meant that in practice very few African Americans voted. In 1870, the Fifteenth Amendment gave African American men the right to vote. As a result, hundreds of thousands of recently freed slaves in the South registered to vote.

African American Men Yet the right to vote for African American citizens was strongly resisted in the South. By

The Privilege of Voting

Voting is probably the most effective means of holding elected officials accountable for their actions. Nevertheless, it is not considered a natural right of a free people, as are the rights of freedom of speech, freedom of religion, or freedom of assembly. Indeed, in the early years of the nation, only men over the age of 21 who owned property could vote. As long ago as 1875, the Supreme Court acknowledged that voting is a privilege, not a right, when in the case of *Minor v. Happersett* it declared that:

Certainly, if the courts can consider any question settled, this is one. For nearly ninety years the people have acted upon the idea that the Consti-

tution, when it conferred citizenship, did not necessarily confer the right of suffrage [voting].

Voting is a privilege to be enjoyed by those who meet the conditions specified by the laws governing voting. In the past, various requirements were established by every state, and these requirements had to be met before a person could vote. Today, most of the requirements have been dropped, but some requirements still must be met. Other than citizenship, probably the most common requirement is residency in the state for a period of time. Today, an increasing number of Americans are eligible to vote because of the actions of the federal government.

V–W

the 1890s, many Southern states had amended their constitutions and enacted a series of laws to prevent African Americans from voting. As a result, by 1910, nearly all African Americans in the South had lost the right to vote. It was not until 1965 that Congress passed the Voting Rights Act to guarantee African Americans the rights granted to them by the Fifteenth Amendment.

Women Many American women were encouraged by the Fifteenth Amendment and hoped that it would also include them. Yet when women's rights activist Susan B. Anthony tried to vote in the 1872 presidential election, she was arrested and fined. Six years later, in 1878, Anthony and Elizabeth Cady Stanton, another prominent women's rights leader, wrote a woman suffrage amendment. It was introduced to Congress that year but was defeated. However, the Woman Suffrage's Amendment was reintroduced into every session of Congress for the next 40 years, until it finally passed in 1920 as the Nineteenth Amendment.

Native Americans In 1924, Native Americans were first granted U.S. citizenship by the passage of the Indian Citizenship Act, and with it, they were granted the right to vote. However, though all Native Americans were now citizens, not all states wanted to allow them to vote. Western states, in particular, passed various laws to keep Native Americans from voting. It was not until the 1940s that the last three states—Maine, Arizona, and New Mexico—finally granted the right to vote to Native Americans.

EXPANDING SUFFRAGE
Because Washington, D.C., the nation's capital, is not part of any state, and the states establish their own voting qualifications, residents there did not have the right to vote in presidential elections until the Twenty-third Amendment was passed in 1961. This amendment gave the District of Columbia the same number of electors in the Electoral College as if it were a state. Thus, Washington, D.C., citizens could vote for president.

Ending Poll Taxes In 1964, the Twenty-fourth Amendment to the U.S. Constitution prohibited **poll taxes** in all federal elections. Poll taxes, or taxes required for voter registration, had been enacted in 11 Southern states after Reconstruction simply to prevent African Americans and poor whites from voting, because they often could not pay the tax. Now a person's income could no longer be a restriction for voting.

New, Sweeping Legislation The following year, the Voting Rights Act was signed into law by President Lyndon B. Johnson (1963–1969). Many consider the Voting Rights Act the most successful law to protect the rights of African Americans ever passed by Congress. The act prohibited any American citizen from being denied the right to vote. It also allowed for federal observers to monitor suspect polling places to ensure that no one was interfering with registration and voting.

In 1971, the Twenty-sixth Amendment lowered the voting age from 21 to 18. The amendment was adopted in response to student activism against the Vietnam War. It lowered the voting age to match the draft age.

Finally, in 1993, Congress passed the National Voter Registration Act, which changed the voter registration procedures for federal elections. The law was designed to make voter registration easier in order to increase voter turnout for elections.

See also: Electoral College System; Voting Rights Act (1965).

FURTHER READING

Keyssar, Alexander. *The Right to Vote: The Contested History of Democracy in the United States.* New York: Basic Books, 2000.

Voting Rights Act (1965)

Major legislation that enforced the guarantees spelled out in the Fifteenth Amendment (1870), ensuring African Americans' right to vote. The act makes certain that African American citizens are full participants in the nation's **federal** system.

The Voting Rights Act of 1965 closed several loopholes in earlier laws designed to end discrimination at the polls. It is considered one of the most significant laws ever passed by Congress; it firmly established the federal government's right to ensure electoral fairness. Congress has extended the provisions of the law several times, most recently in 2006.

CIVIL RIGHTS IN THE 1950S AND EARLY 1960S

As the civil rights movement began to gather force in the 1950s, the Eisenhower administration (1953–1961) urged Congress to use federal power to ensure the voting rights of black citizens. Congress's first action was passage of the Civil Rights Act of 1957.

The 1957 act authorized the attorney general to bring lawsuits to stop any obstruction with the right of black people to vote. The law also created the Civil Rights Commission to investigate problems of racial discrimination, such as being denied the right to vote.

Congress then passed the Civil Rights Act of 1964, requiring the states to adopt standard procedures for all persons seeking to register to vote. The law also required local officials to justify rejecting an applicant who had completed the sixth grade.

SLOW PROGRESS

Yet progress remained slow. On March 8, 1965, the Reverend Martin Luther King, Jr., led a "Walk for Freedom" to dramatize the need for additional efforts on behalf of registering African American voters in Selma, Alabama, and elsewhere in the South. The violent reaction of local white law enforcement officers and white bystanders to the peaceful demonstration drew nationwide attention to the problem.

THE PRESIDENT ACTS

A week later, President Lyndon B. Johnson (1963–1969) addressed a

V–
W

History Speaks

The American Promise

Throughout the 1950s and early 1960s, many Southern blacks were prevented from voting. After the 1964 election, several civil rights groups joined forces to work for African-American voting rights. President Lyndon B. Johnson (1963–1969), in a joint-session address to Congress, called for a strong voting rights bill to enforce the Fourteenth and Fifteenth Amendments.

Mr. Speaker, Mr. President, Members of the Congress:

I speak tonight for the dignity of man and the destiny of democracy. . . .

Rarely are we met with a challenge, not to our growth or abundance, our welfare or our security, but rather to the values and the purposes and the meaning of our beloved Nation.

The issue of equal rights for American Negroes is such an issue. And should we defeat every enemy, should we double our wealth and conquer the stars, and still be unequal to this issue, then we will have failed as a people and as a nation. . . .

There is no Negro problem. There is no Southern problem. There is no Northern problem. There is only an American problem. And we are met here tonight as Americans—not as Democrats or Republicans—we are met here as Americans to solve that problem. . . .

Many of the issues of civil rights are very complex and most difficult. But about this there can and should be no argument. Every American citizen must have an equal right to vote. There is no reason which can excuse the denial of that right. There is no duty which weighs more heavily on us than the duty we have to ensure that right.

Yet the harsh fact is that in many places in this country men and women are kept from voting simply because they are Negroes. . . .

In such a case our duty must be clear to all of us. The Constitution says that no person shall be kept from voting because of his race or his color. We have all sworn an oath before God to support and to defend that Constitution. We must now act in obedience to that oath.

There is no constitutional issue here. The command of the Constitution is plain.

There is no moral issue. It is wrong—deadly wrong—to deny any of your fellow Americans the right to vote in this country.

There is no issue of States rights or national rights. There is only the struggle for human rights. . . .

President Johnson forcefully addressed Congress on March 15, 1965. He called for legislation to guarantee African Americans the right to vote, and he signed the bill into law on August 6, 1965. The new law strengthened the federal government's power concerning voting rights.

V– W

joint session of Congress to ask for passage of a new voting rights measure. Johnson explained that "no law that we now have on the books . . . can ensure the right to vote when local officials are determined to deny it." Within five months, Congress had approved the sweeping Voting Rights Act of 1965.

The law ended **literacy tests.** It also provided for the appointment of federal supervisors of voter registration. Passage of the Voting Rights Act brought a significant increase in the number of African Americans registered to vote. Within four years, almost one million blacks had registered to vote under its provisions.

The Civil Rights Commission reported in 1968 that registration of African Americans had climbed to more than 50 percent of the black voting-age population in every Southern state. Before the act, African American registration had exceeded 50 percent in only three states—Florida, Tennessee, and Texas. The most dramatic increase occurred in Mississippi. African American registration in that state rose from 6.7 percent to 59.8 percent of the voting-age population.

VOTING LAW EXTENDED

In 1970, the Voting Rights Act was renewed for an additional five years. Supporters of the law turned back the efforts of Southern senators who wished to weaken key provisions. State and local governments were forbidden to use literacy tests or other voter-qualifying devices.

By the time the act was due for its second extension in 1975, an estimated 2 million African Americans had been added to the voting rolls in the South, more than doubling the previous total. The number of African Americans holding elective office also increased significantly.

The Voting Rights Act was renewed for seven years and expanded in 1975. Two additional provisions gave greater protection to certain language minorities, defined as persons of Hispanic heritage, Native Americans, Asian Americans, and Alaska Natives.

These amendments significantly expanded coverage of the Voting Rights Act. In addition, provisions were added requiring certain parts of the country to provide bilingual voting materials.

GROWING CONGRESSIONAL SUPPORT

Congress approved a third extension of the act on June 23, 1982, two months before the law was due to expire. The 1982 legislation represented a major victory for civil rights groups that included African American, Hispanic, labor, religious, and civic organizations. The bill received widespread bipartisan support and strong backing from members of both chambers of Congress, including Southerners. More than twice as many Southern Democrats in both the **Senate** and House voted for passage in 1982 than in 1965 when the law was first approved. The steady upward trend in Southern support for the act reflected changing social and political views as well as a great increase in black voting in the South.

In July 2006, President George W. Bush (2001–2009) signed another 25-year extension of the Voting Rights Act. The act extends prohibition against the use of tests or devices to deny the right to vote in any federal, state, or local election. It also extends the requirement for certain states and local governments to provide voting materials in multiple languages. During the signing ceremony, Bush noted,

> My administration will vigorously enforce the provisions of this law, and we will defend it in court. This legislation is named in honor of three heroes of American history who devoted their lives to the struggle of civil rights: Fannie Lou Hamer, Rosa Parks, and Coretta Scott King. And in honor of their memory and their contributions to the cause of freedom, I am proud to sign the Voting Rights Act Reauthorization and Amendments Act of 2006.

JUDICIAL SUPPORT

Not surprisingly, the use of federal power over electoral and voting matters included in the Voting Rights Act was challenged as exceeding the constitutional authority of Congress and infringing on states' rights. Primarily, these challenges came from the South. In 1966, however, the Supreme Court firmly backed the power of Congress to pass such a law.

The Supreme Court rejected all constitutional challenges to the act. "Congress," wrote Chief Justice Earl Warren for the decision's 8–1 majority, "has full remedial powers [under the Fifteenth Amendment] to effectuate the constitutional prohibition against racial discrimination in voting." The federal approval requirement for new voting rules in the states covered by the act, Warren observed, "may have been an uncommon exercise of congressional power . . . but the Court has recognized that exceptional conditions can justify legislative measures not otherwise appropriate." Thus, the Voting Rights Act and the court decisions supporting it made it clear that voting is a federal, and not a state, responsibility.

See also: States' Rights; Voter Registration.

FURTHER READING

American Government at Work, Volume 1: The Federal Legislative Branch. Danbury, Conn.: Grolier/Scholastic Library, 2001.

Branch, Taylor. *Pillar of Fire: America in the King Years, 1963–1965.* New York: Simon & Schuster, 1999.

Finlayson, Reggie. *We Shall Overcome: The History of the American Civil Rights Movement.* Minneapolis, Minn.: Lerner Books, 2002.

Hardy, Sheila Jackson, and P. Stephen Hardy. *Extraordinary People of the Civil Rights Movement.* New York: Children's Press, 2007.

Williams, Juan. *Eyes on the Prize: America's Civil Rights Years, 1954–1965.* New York: Penguin Books, 1988.

Washington, D.C.

See Federal City: Washington, D.C.

Washington, George (1732–1799)

Commander-in-chief of the Continental Army during the American Revolution (1775–1783) and first president of the United States. George Washington also served as the president of the Constitutional Convention in 1787, which established the nation's **federal** system of government.

EARLY LIFE

George Washington was born on February 22, 1732, on Pope's Creek Estate, near present-day Colonial Beach, Virginia. He was homeschooled by his father in the classics, math, and land surveying. Washington's father died in 1743. Washington was then sent to live with his half brother, Lawrence, at Mount Vernon, an estate owned by his half brother's family, the Fairfaxes. Lawrence had married into upper-class society, and so he brought his younger brother into a world of education and manners. Because of his experience with surveying, Washington got a job surveying Lord Fairfax's estate in the Shenandoah Valley, in Virginia, in 1748. Lord Fairfax then used his influence to get Washington a job as a surveyor for Culpeper County. Washington also

V–W

helped with the city planning of Belhaven, Virginia, now called Alexandria.

In 1752, Lawrence died, and the Mount Vernon estate passed to Washington, who believed farming to be an honorable and profitable profession. He expanded the estate and sunk his efforts into turning Mount Vernon into a thriving business. To run his plantation, Washington used slaves, although he wished the institution was not necessary and made provisions in his will for his slaves to be either cared for in their old age or freed. Because Washington disliked breaking up slave families, he kept and supported more slaves than his estate required.

Washington was an outdoorsman and a gentleman. He was well liked in the community and interested in public affairs. He even expressed an interest in joining the House of Burgesses, the governing body of the Virginia **colony**.

MILITARY CAREER

At about the same time that he became the owner of Mount Vernon, Washington also became an officer in the Virginia militia. As tensions with the French rose, Washington was dispatched by the governor of Virginia to inform the French that they should leave the Ohio River valley or they would be forced out. The trip was a difficult one, and Washington nearly froze to death after falling into an icy river.

The French refused to leave, leading to the French and Indian War (1754–1763), in which the British fought the French and their Indian allies. Washington had a distinguished career during the war and left the military as commander of all of Virginia's forces. He returned to Mount Vernon to resume running his plantation.

Marriage In 1759, Washington married Martha Dandridge Custis, a wealthy widow. They had known each other only three weeks at the time of their marriage. Martha brought about 15,000 acres (60 km^2) of land and two children to the marriage. George and Martha never had children, but Washington doted on his adopted children as if they were his own.

Farmer and Public Service From 1759 to 1775, Washington was an active and innovative farmer and participant in public life. As he had planned, he joined the House of Burgesses in 1759. Washington put considerable effort into the development of his plantation, building his enterprise into a self-sufficient community. Not until Patrick Henry read his Virginia Stamp Act Resolutions before the House of Burgesses, however, did Washington start to take part in the move for independence. He participated in the First Continental Congress and pledged to raise an army of his own for the cause. He had quickly become convinced that letters and pleas would not resolve the problems between Britain and the colonies.

ROLE IN THE REVOLUTION

Washington's most famous contribution to American independence was as the commander-in-chief of the

Continental Army in the Revolutionary War (1775–1783). It was an almost impossible job. American militia were fighting one of the most powerful and experienced militaries in the world. The American forces had irregular supplies, untrained officers, and no money. Often, the Continental Army had no food. Washington's leadership is credited with winning the Revolution, as he often had nothing more than inspiring speeches and personal charisma keeping his army together.

Following the Americans' victory in the war, Washington returned to his estate at Mount Vernon, although that stay was short-lived. It was becoming clear that the newly independent nation was foundering. The nation's first government, the Articles of Confederation (1781–1788), was a weak central government with little authority over the states. Rather than see his wartime efforts go to waste, Washington continually wrote to the leading **Patriots** urging them toward a solution. Despite seeing the need for a strong central government, Washington himself did not wish to attend a convention or be involved in restructuring the country. When he was asked to attend the Constitutional Convention, where the nation's leaders planned to strengthen or replace the weak Articles of Confederation, he reluctantly agreed.

THE CONVENTION

Washington was elected unanimously to preside over the convention. While he said little throughout the debates, he believed that the resolutions to the problems of the Articles of Confederation needed deep and thoughtful contemplation. The convention would be a failure if it could not precisely identify and fix the weaknesses in the government. Simple solutions and quick patches would not do.

The weight of Washington's opinion was heavy on the delegates, and his support of the new Constitution convinced many to vote for its adoption. Following that, his personal appeals to the politicians of the states helped secure **ratification** of the new government by the states.

FIRST PRESIDENT

Considering his efforts on behalf of the nation complete, Washington was prepared to again return to Mount Vernon. Yet there was no other choice for the first president. He commanded respect from every part of the nation. He had international renown. He was the only indisputable choice. And again, reluctantly, he accepted his nation's call to service.

Washington's administration (1789–1797) was marked by careful deliberation and cautious action. He maintained balance between the Federalists and anti-Federalists in his Cabinet. A Southerner, he toured the North first, then the South, to show that he was the country's president, not the president of only the area he called his home. Slowly, Washington came to support Federalist causes, such as establishing a national bank, because these would benefit the nation as a whole. Washington strove to maintain **neutrality** in foreign affairs to show the world that the young United States would maintain its own dignity.

V– W

After serving two terms, and truly wishing to retire from public life, Washington refused a third term in office, thus establishing the presidential tradition of serving two terms. He returned to Mount Vernon in 1797 and lived another two years, dying on December 14, 1799.

See also: Articles of Confederation; Constitutional Convention; Henry, Patrick.

FURTHER READING

Brookhiser, Richard. *Founding Father.* New York: Free Press, 1996.

Calkhoven, Laurie. *George Washington: An American Life.* New York: Sterling Books, 2007.

Johnson, Paul. *George Washington: The Founding Father.* New York: HarperCollins, 2005.

Webster, Daniel (1782–1852)

Famous politician and orator of the Antebellum Period, the era before the Civil War (1861–1865). Daniel Webster was a strong supporter of the national government.

EARLY LIFE AND CAREER

Daniel Webster was born on January 18, 1782, in Salisbury, New Hampshire, one of 10 children. His parents owned a small farm, and all of the children except Daniel worked as farmhands. Because young Daniel was sickly, he was not allowed to participate in the strenuous work.

His family taught him to read at home. At age 14, he attended the Phillips Exeter Academy. At 15, he was accepted to Dartmouth College. Webster was an excellent student and joined Phi Beta Kappa, an academic honors society.

Law Career After graduating from Dartmouth in 1801, Webster began to work and study with Thomas W. Thompson, a lawyer. Because of financial hardships at home, Webster briefly quit his law studies and worked as a schoolteacher. In 1804, Webster moved to Boston to work for a prominent lawyer, Christopher Gore. Because of Gore's practice and personal interest in politics, Webster came into contact with a number of politicians.

Supporting the Federalists In 1805, Webster passed the bar exam and returned home to New Hampshire to start his own law practice. He also took on a number of speaking engagements, having found that he was well suited to public speaking. Politically, Webster was a Federalist, so he often spoke out in support of Federalist causes. In 1807, President Thomas Jefferson (1801–1809) pushed the Embargo Act, which cut off trade between the United States and **Great Britain** and France. In turn, Webster wrote a pamphlet protesting the measure because the embargo hurt Northern merchants.

EARLY POLITICAL CAREER

The tensions between the United States and Britain finally exploded into the War of 1812 (1812–1814). While he denounced the war and the embargo that had hurt the North, he also strongly supported the Union.

Some legislators in the New England states threatened secession, but Webster opposed such extreme and destructive measures.

Because of his persuasiveness, he was asked to help draft a list of grievances on behalf of New Englanders to President James Madison (1809–1817). In 1812, Webster was elected to the House of Representatives from the state of New Hampshire. He remained a member of the House for two terms, before returning to his law practice.

In 1827, Webster was elected to the **Senate** from Massachusetts. While in the Senate, he supported the Tariff of 1828. The South, however, strongly opposed this **tariff** because it raised prices on overseas goods. Turmoil in the South led to the Nullification Crisis. This threat to the nation's unity was led by South Carolina's John C. Calhoun, who was at the time Andrew Jackson's (1829–1837) vice president. Calhoun and his supporters argued that a state had the right to **nullify** any **federal** law that threatened its interests. The legislature of South Carolina threatened to vote to **secede** from the Union if its demands were not met. Webster threw his support behind President Jackson and helped bring the Nullification Crisis to an end by supporting a compromise tariff.

LATER YEARS

Webster remained active in the Senate. He was a leader of the Whig Party, which opposed Jackson and the Democratic Party. Later, in 1850, following the Mexican War (1846–1848) and the **annexation** of land from Mexico, Webster again supported efforts to keep the Union whole. Northerners argued that slavery should not be allowed to expand into the newly acquired lands. In response, Southerners claimed that Congress could not regulate the expansion of slavery.

In turn, Senator Henry Clay of Kentucky proposed the Compromise of 1850. Webster supported this series of laws because he believed the Western lands were fundamentally unsuited for plantation farming. Even if slavery were allowed, the argument went, there would be little need or use for slaves. The compromise, however, would calm the slave states and preserve the Union. **Abolitionists** later characterized Webster as a man lacking moral character because among the items in the compromise was the severe Fugitive Slave Law, which required Northerners to return escaped slaves.

However, the Compromise of 1850 only forestalled the inevitable. The tensions between slave and free states were temporarily defused, but 11 years later, the country would find itself torn by the Civil War (1861–1865).

See also: Calhoun, John C.; Clay, Henry; Compromise of 1850; Jackson, Andrew; States' Rights.

FURTHER READING

Harvey, Bonnie C. *Daniel Webster: Liberty and Union, Now and Forever.* Berkeley Heights, N.J.: Enslow Publishers, 2001.

Remini, Robert V. *Daniel Webster: The Man and His Time.* New York: W.W. Norton & Company, 1997.

**V–
W**

Whiskey Rebellion (1794)

A series of attacks by farmers against tax agents in western Pennsylvania to protest a tax on whiskey imposed by the **federal** government. The Whiskey Rebellion was the first test of power of the new federal government under the U.S. Constitution. It demonstrated that central power could override the power of individual states.

By 1790, the new federal government of the United States, as established by the Constitution, had assumed responsibility for all the war debts the colonies amassed during the American Revolution (1775–1783). This left the government with a huge debt. In 1791, Secretary of the Treasury Alexander Hamilton proposed a bill that would add an **excise tax** to all distilled spirits, or alcoholic beverages that are made from grain or fruit, such as whiskey and wine. Both houses of Congress approved the bill.

PROTESTS

Whiskey producers all over the country protested this bill. The strongest protests, however, came from the **frontier** regions of the country, which included the western counties of Pennsylvania. Because it was difficult to transport goods over the Appalachian Mountains to the cities in the East, it was most practical for frontier farmers to transport and sell the grain they had grown as distilled whiskey, instead of as raw grain. By shipping whiskey, however, they would be required to pay an excise tax on their main crop.

Large producers of whiskey were allowed to make an annual tax payment, and the more whiskey they produced, the lower the excise tax was. Yet smaller producers, like those frontier farmers who only made whiskey occasionally, had to make payments throughout the year, and the tax worked out to be greater for them. Thus, they felt the new tax gave large producers a greater competitive advantage. Furthermore, the excise tax was only payable in cash, which was rare on the frontier. Most frontier farmers used whiskey to pay for goods and services they needed.

GROWING DISCONTENT

The farmers in the western counties were not eager to pay an excise tax supporting a national government that they believed did not represent them well. Although many American citizens in the East supported decisions made by the federal government, people on the western frontier were less accepting of the national government, believing instead that only their state government mattered.

Because the farmers of western Pennsylvania felt they were not being well represented by Congress in distant New York, then the nation's capital, they decided to establish their own assembly to deal with the matter of the excise tax. Each county was to choose between three and five representatives, and these people were to bring the demands of their county to the assembly. Many of the representatives felt hostile toward the national government, and some of the more radical members advocated violence.

At one committee meeting held in Pittsburgh in August 1792, the group of representatives drafted a report that began by stating that they were "convinced that a tax upon liquors which are the common drink of a nation operates in proportion to the number and not to the wealth of the people, and of course is unjust in itself, and oppressive upon the poor." Many frontier farmers considered the tax on whiskey similar to the stamp tax that Britain had imposed on the American colonists in 1765 and which ultimately led to revolution.

Most western farmers simply refused to pay the tax, but others reacted with violence toward excise officers. These were men sent to each county to open an office where they could collect the excise tax. Often, rebellious farmers threatened people who offered to house the excise officer and sometimes threatened the excise officer himself. These threats were usually enough to discourage the officer from staying and trying to collect the tax.

FEDERAL REACTION

In response to this resistance, President George Washington (1789–1797) issued a proclamation in September 1792 condemning those who had interfered with the collection of the tax. However, violence continued to grow over the next two years. Violence was most prevalent in four counties in western Pennsylvania—Allegheny, Fayette, Washington, and Westmoreland—where a large number of distilleries were located.

VIOLENCE ERUPTS

In July 1794, U.S. Marshal David Lennon came to western Pennsylvania to order those farmers who had not paid the whiskey tax to appear in federal court in Philadelphia. On July 15, Lennon and Washington County collector John Neville were met by an armed group of men as they tried to serve papers to a farmer in the county. Shots were fired, but no one was injured. The following day an angry mob marched on John Neville's house, had a shootout with him, and eventually burned his home. Violence soon spread to the other western counties. Rebels burned the home of Benjamin Wells, the collector for Fayette County, and then stole the mail from a post rider leaving Pittsburgh to see who in the local area opposed the rebels. At the same time, about 7,000 frontiersmen marched on Pittsburgh to stop collection of the tax.

Calling Out the Militia On August 7, 1794, President Washington issued a proclamation, calling out the militia and ordering the western farmers to return to their homes. This was the first use of the Militia Law of 1792, which allowed the president to use the militia to "suppress insurrections" in one state by using troops from other states. Washington's proclamation mobilized an army of approximately 13,000 men from

V–W

Determined to see the nation's federal system succeed, Washington personally led the American militia against the rebellious farmers of western Pennsylvania, in what became known as the Whiskey Rebellion.

Maryland, New Jersey, Pennsylvania, and Virginia.

In a last attempt to avoid confrontation, Washington sent members of his Cabinet, including Attorney General William Bradford, to meet with the rebel leaders, but no peaceful solution could be reached. By September, the group returned to Philadelphia and reported that it was necessary to send out the militia in order to ensure that the laws would be carried out.

Leading the Troops To assert his presidential authority, Washington himself led the troops to western Pennsylvania. On September 25, he issued a proclamation that stated he would not "allow a small portion of the United States [to] dictate to the whole union." By October, the uprising collapsed because of the overwhelming force of the troops. In the end, about 20 rebels were arrested and sent to Philadelphia to trial. All were ultimately pardoned by Washington. The Whiskey Rebellion had proven that the new government would and could enforce laws enacted by Congress in the face of rebellion.

See also: States' Rights; Washington, George.

FURTHER READING

Burns, James MacGregor, and Susan Dunn. *George Washington*. New York: Times Books, 2004.

Evernden, Margery. *Wilderness Boy.* Pittsburgh, Pa.: University of Pittsburgh Press, 2001.

Hogeland, William. *The Whiskey Rebellion: George Washington, Alexander Hamilton, and the Frontier Rebels Who Challenged America's Newfound Sovereignty.* New York: Scribner, 2006.

Schiel, Katy. *The Whiskey Rebellion: An Early Challenge to America's New Government.* New York: Rosen Publishing Group, 2003.

V–W

Viewpoints About Federalism

Farewell Address, George Washington, 1796

Although George Washington's (1789–1796) farewell address is one of his most famous speeches, it was never actually delivered by the president. He arranged for it to be published in a Philadelphia newspaper. In his address, Washington announces his upcoming retirement from politics "after forty-five years of my life dedicated to [the nation's] service." Later, he goes on to extol the benefits of the **federal**, or central, government to the people.

> ... The unity of government which constitutes you one people is also now dear to you. It is justly so, for it is a main pillar in the edifice of your real independence, the support of your tranquility at home, your peace abroad; of your safety; of your prosperity; of that very liberty which you so highly prize. But as it is easy to foresee that, from different causes and from different quarters, much pains will be taken, many artifices employed to weaken in your minds the conviction of this truth; as this is the point in your political fortress against which the batteries of internal and external enemies will be most constantly and actively (though often covertly and insidiously) directed, it is of infinite moment that you should properly estimate the immense value of your national union to your collective and individual happiness; that you should cherish a cordial, habitual, and immovable attachment to it; accustoming yourselves to think and speak of it as of the palladium of your political safety and prosperity; watching for its preservation with jealous anxiety; discountenancing whatever may suggest even a suspicion that it can in any event be abandoned; and indignantly frowning upon the first dawning of every attempt to alienate any portion of our country from the rest, or to enfeeble the sacred ties which now link together the various parts.

Inaugural Address, John Adams, 1797

Upon assuming office as the nation's second president, John Adams (1797–1801) gave his inaugural address to the people of the young nation on March 4, 1797. In his speech, he praises the U.S. Constitution and talks about the **federal** relationship of sharing power between the national and the state governments.

> " . . . I first saw the Constitution of the United States in a foreign country. . . . I read it with great satisfaction, as the result of good heads prompted by good hearts, as an experiment better adapted to the genius, character, situation, and relations of this nation and country than any which had ever been proposed or suggested. In its general principles and great outlines it was conformable to such a system of government as I had ever most esteemed, and in some States, my own native State in particular, had contributed to establish. Claiming a right of suffrage, in common with my fellow-citizens, in the adoption or rejection of a constitution which was to rule me and my posterity, as well as them and theirs, I did not hesitate to express my approbation [approval] of it on all occasions, in public and in private. It was not then, nor has been since, any objection to it in my mind that the Executive and Senate were not more permanent. Nor have I ever entertained a thought of promoting any alteration in it but such as the people themselves, in the course of their experience, should see and feel to be necessary or expedient, and by their representatives in Congress and the State legislatures, according to the Constitution itself, adopt and ordain. . . .
>
> What other form of government, indeed, can so well deserve our esteem and love? . . . "

❗ *Inaugural Address, Thomas Jefferson, 1801*

The presidential election of 1800 marked a unique experience in history: Political power had passed peacefully from one party to the other. Federalist John Adams (1797–1801) lost reelection, and Republican Thomas Jefferson (1801–1809) succeeded him. In his inaugural address, presented to the nation on March 4, 1801, Jefferson reaches out to Federalists and praises the democratic principles embodied in the United States Constitution.

Although a strict constructionist who opposed many of the policies of the Federalist Party, President Jefferson nonetheless reached out to the Federalists in 1801 and urged cooperation in his first Inaugural Address.

" . . . During the contest of opinion [presidential election of 1800] through which we have passed the animation of discussions and of exertions has sometimes worn an aspect which might impose on strangers unused to think freely and to speak and to write what they think; but this being now decided by the voice of the nation, announced according to the rules of the Constitution, all will, of course, arrange themselves under the will of the law, and unite in common efforts for the common good. All, too, will bear in mind this sacred principle, that though the will of the majority is in all cases to prevail, that will to be rightful must be reasonable; that the minority possess their equal rights, which equal law must protect, and to violate would be oppression. Let us, then, fellow-citizens, unite with one heart and one mind. . . . But every difference of opinion is not a difference of principle. We have called by different names brethren of the same principle. We are all Republicans, we are all Federalists. If there be any among us who would wish to dissolve this Union or to change its republican form, let them stand undisturbed as monuments of the safety with which error of opinion may be tolerated where reason is left free to combat it. I know, indeed, that some honest men fear that a republican government can not be strong, that this Government is not strong enough; but would the honest patriot, in the full tide of successful experiment, abandon a government which has so far kept us free and firm on the theoretic and visionary fear that this Government, the world's best hope, may by possibility want energy to preserve itself? I trust not. I believe this, on the contrary, the strongest Government on earth. . . .

Let us, then, with courage and confidence pursue our own Federal and Republican principles, our attachment to union and representative government. . . . Still one thing more, fellow-citizens—a wise and frugal Government, which shall restrain men from injuring one another, shall leave them otherwise free to regulate their own pursuits of industry and improvement, and shall not take from the mouth of labor the bread it has earned. This is the sum of good government, and this is necessary to close the circle of our felicities [happiness]. "

✹ McCulloch v. Maryland, 1819

In a unanimous decision in *McCulloch v. Maryland,*
the U.S. Supreme Court held that Congress had the
power to incorporate the bank and that Maryland
could not tax organizations of the national government, such as the Bank of the United States, used in
the execution of the government's constitutional
powers. Writing for the Court, Chief Justice Marshall noted that Congress possessed unenumerated
powers, that is, powers not explicitly called out in
the Constitution.

Marshall also held that while the states retained
the power of taxation, "the constitution and the
laws made in pursuance thereof are supreme . . . they
control the constitution and laws of the respective
states." Thus, the Court upheld the principle of federalism, of a shared role in government, noting that
some rights and powers are reserved to the states,
while others belong to the national government.

> ❝ The question submitted to the court for their decision in this case, is, as to the validity of the said act of the general assembly of Maryland, on the ground of its being repugnant to the constitution of the United States, and the act of congress aforesaid, or to one of them. . . .
>
> The first question has, for many years, divided the opinions of the first men of our country. He did not mean to controvert the arguments by which the bank was maintained, on its original establishment. The power may now be denied, in perfect consistency with those arguments. It is agreed, that no such power is expressly granted by the constitution. It has been obtained by implication; by reasoning from the 8th section of the 1st article of the constitution; and asserted to exist, not of and by itself, but as an appendage to other granted powers, as necessary to carry them into execution. If the bank be not 'necessary and proper' for this purpose, it has no foundation in our constitution, and can have no support in this court. But it strikes us, at once, that a power, growing out of a necessity which may not be permanent, may also not be permanent. It has relation to circumstances which change; in a state of things which may exist at one period, and not at another. The argument might have been perfectly good, to show the necessity of a bank, for the operations of the revenue, in 1791, and entirely

fail now, when so many facilities for money transactions abound, which were wanting then. . . .

The power to establish such a corporation [a national bank] is implied, and involved in the grant of specific powers in the constitution; because the end involves the means necessary to carry it into effect. A power without the means to use it, is a nullity. But we are not driven to seek for this power in implication: because the constitution, after enumerating certain specific powers, expressly gives to congress the power 'to make all laws which shall be necessary and proper for carrying into execution the foregoing powers, and all other powers vested by this constitution in the government of the United States, or in any department or officer thereof.' If, therefore, the act of congress establishing the bank was necessary and proper to carry into execution any one or more of the enumerated powers, the authority to pass it is expressly delegated to congress by the constitution. We contend, that it was necessary and proper to carry into execution several of the enumerated powers, such as the powers of levying and collecting taxes throughout this widely-extended empire; of paying the public debts, both in the United States and in foreign countries; of borrowing money, at home and abroad; of regulating commerce with foreign nations, and among the several states; of raising and supporting armies and a navy; and of carrying on war. That banks, dispersed throughout the country, are appropriate means of carrying into execution all these powers, cannot be denied. Our history furnishes abundant experience of the utility of a national bank as an instrument of finance. . . .

The only remaining question is, whether the act of the state of Maryland, for taxing the bank thus incorporated, be repugnant to the constitution of the United States? We insist, that any such tax, by authority of a state, would be unconstitutional, and that this act is so, from its peculiar provisions. . . . There is another clause in the constitution, which has the effect of a prohibition on the exercise of their authority, in numerous cases. The 6th article of the constitution of the United States declares, that the laws made in pursuance of it, 'shall be the supreme law of the land, anything in the constitution, or laws of any state to the contrary notwithstanding.' By this declaration, the states are prohibited from passing any acts which shall be repugnant to a law of the United States.

99

Richard Nixon's Campaign Speech to Visit All 50 States, 1960

In 1960, Vice President Richard Nixon was the Republican Party's nominee for the presidency. In his speech accepting the nomination, the vice president pledged to campaign in all 50 states. In this excerpt from an August 26, 1960, campaign speech in Alabama, Nixon notes the importance of the states and calls for all presidential candidates to campaign in all 50 states. In this particular speech, of course, Nixon, a Republican, was trying to convince the voters of Alabama, who had always voted for the Democratic candidate, to switch and vote for the Republican ticket.

" A few days ago when we announced that we were going to be able to visit Alabama on this trip an individual came up to me who was interested in our success in this campaign and he said: "Mr. Vice President, why are you going down there?" He said: "If President Eisenhower, who is the most popular man ever to run for President in this century, who got the biggest majority that any President ever got—9 million votes in 1956—if he couldn't carry Alabama, why are you going to Alabama? . . ."

I did a little studying after that. I checked to see what had happened in Alabama in the last 30 years. In those 30 years not one Democratic candidate for the Presidency has bothered to come to Alabama to campaign.

As a matter of fact I am proud to say that in those 30 years the only candidate to come to Alabama to campaign was President Dwight Eisenhower in 1952.

And I want to say to you today that I think that situation is wrong. It's wrong for Alabama and it isn't good for the United States. It's wrong, it seems to me, that a situation has existed for 30 years that the candidate of one party didn't find it necessary to come at all and the candidate of the other came only once.

And so I say it's time for a change. It's time for the Democratic candidate for the Presidency to quit taking Alabama and the South for granted.

Just to keep this on a good bipartisan level, it's time for the Republican candidate for the Presidency to quit conceding Alabama and the South to the Democratic candidate.

I announced—as you may recall in my acceptance speech—I announced that I was going to go to every one of the 50 States in this campaign. And certainly, if Pat can hold out, and she's stronger than I am, we're going to make it. And I want to tell you that I hope that all future candidates for the Presidency of both parties will carry their campaigns to every one of the 50 States.

I believe this is in the best interest of the States. I think it's in the best interests of the country. And I believe that it is essential that the people of this State—the people of all the Southern States, the people of all the Nation—exercise the right of choice—a choice between the candidate of the one party, the Democratic Party, and the candidate of the other party, the Republican Party, for the Presidency. And to exercise that choice you've got to hear 'em. You have to see 'em. You have to know what they stand for. . . .

And so I say to you today—I say to those of you who are Republicans—don't vote for me simply because I happen to be in the same party. To those of you who are Democrats I say: Don't vote simply for your party label. I say to all of you: Vote not as Republicans, not as Democrats, but as Americans. Don't vote on the basis of age, of personality, or religion, or party labels, but select the man who agrees with you on the great issues confronting America and the world.

This is what America needs. This is the message that I am carrying to every State in this Union, North, South, and East and West. Vote on the basis of the issues, not on the label, not on the other matters which do not matter as much as do the issues themselves.

”

❗ *State of the Union Address, Ronald Reagan, 1982*

In January 1982, President Ronald Reagan (1981–1989) addressed Congress and the nation with his first State of the Union Address. In his speech, the president called for new programs that reduced the amount of **federal** influence in state and local governments, thus restoring the balance of federalism, or sharing of power, between the national and state governments.

" Today marks my first State of the Union address to you, a constitutional duty as old as our Republic itself. . . .

When I visited this chamber last year as a newcomer to Washington, critical of past policies which I believe had failed, I proposed a new spirit of partnership between this Congress and this Administration and between Washington and our state and local governments. . . .

I am confident the economic program we have put into operation will protect the needy while it triggers a recovery that will benefit all Americans. It will stimulate the economy, result in increased savings, and thus provide capital for expansion, mortgages for home building and jobs for the unemployed.

Now that the essentials of that program are in place, our next major undertaking must be a program—just as bold, just as innovative—to make government again accountable to the people, to make our system of federalism work again.

Our citizens feel they have lost control of even the most basic decisions made about the essential services of government, such as schools, welfare, roads, and even garbage collection. They are right.

A maze of interlocking jurisdictions and levels of government confronts average citizens in trying to solve even the simplest of problems. They do not know where to turn for answers, who to hold accountable, who to praise, who to blame, who to vote for or against.

The main reason for this is the overpowering growth of federal grant-in-aid programs during the past few decades.

In 1960, the federal government had 132 categorical grant programs, costing $7 billion. When I took office, there were approximately 500, costing nearly $100 billion—13 programs for energy conservation, 36 for pollution control, 66 for social services and 90 for education. The list goes on and on. Here in Congress, it takes at least 166 committees just to try to keep track of them.

You know and I know that neither the president nor the Congress can properly oversee this jungle of grants-in-aid. Indeed, the growth of these grants has led to a distortion in the vital functions of government. As one Democratic governor put it recently: "The national government should be worrying about arms control, not potholes."

The growth of these federal programs has—in the words of one intergovernmental commission—made the federal government "more pervasive, more intrusive, more unmanageable, more ineffective, more costly, and above all more unaccountable."

Let us solve this problem with a single, bold stroke—the return of some $47 billion in federal programs to state and local government, together with the means to finance them in a transition period of nearly 10 years to avoid disruption. . . .

Starting in fiscal 1984, the federal government will assume full responsibility for the cost of the rapidly growing Medicaid program to go along with its existing responsibility for Medicare. As part of a financially equal swap, the states will simultaneously take full responsibility for Aid to Families with Dependent Children and food stamps. This will make welfare less costly and more responsive to genuine need because it will be designed and administered closer to the grass roots of people it serves.

In 1984, the federal government will apply the full proceeds from certain excise taxes to a grass roots trust fund that will belong, in fair shares, to the 50 states. The total amount flowing into this fund will be $28 billion a year.

Over the next four years, the states can use this money in either of two ways. If they want to continue receiving federal grants in such areas as transportation, education, and social services, they can use their trust fund money to pay for the grants or, to the extent they choose to forego the federal grant programs, they can use their trust fund money on their own, for other purposes. There will be a mandatory pass-through of part of these funds to local governments.

By 1988, the states will be in complete control of over 40 federal grant programs. The trust fund will start to phase out, eventually to disappear, and the excise taxes will then be turned over to the states. They can then preserve, raise or lower taxes on their own and fund and manage these programs as they see fit.

In a single stroke, we will be accomplishing a realignment that will end cumbersome administration and spiraling costs at the federal level while we insure these programs will be more responsive to both the people they are meant to help and the people who pay for them.

Hand in hand with this program to strengthen the discretion and flexibility of state and local governments, we are proposing legislation for an experimental effort to improve and develop our depressed urban areas in the 1980s and 1990s. This legislation will permit states and localities to apply to the federal government for designation as urban enterprise zones. A broad range of special economic incentives in these zones will help attract new business, new jobs, and new opportunity to America's inner cities and rural towns. Some will say our mission is to save free enterprise. I say we must save free enterprise so that, together, we can save America.

"

Glossary of Key Terms

abolitionist(s) A person or persons opposed to slavery and in favor of ending it.

agrarian Related to agriculture and farming.

alien A person living in a country but who is not a citizen of that country.

allies People or countries with whom one has made a pact of mutual support.

amalgamate To combine or unite.

amendment A change to the Constitution.

annexation The addition of territory to an existing nation or state.

aristocracy The upper classes or nobility.

arsenal A collection of weapons.

bankruptcy Inability to pay off a debt.

bicameral A two-house legislature.

Boston Massacre Event in American history in which British soldiers stationed in Boston fired on American colonists, killing five.

Boston Tea Party A protest against the tax policies of Great Britain in which colonists, disguised as Native Americans, boarded ships in Boston Harbor and threw chests of British tea overboard.

checks and balances A system of government in which each branch exercises some control over the others.

colonial government The administration of lands that are dependencies of a powerful parent country.

colony A town or city established in a new land but controlled by a parent country.

commerce Exchange of goods, ideas, or opinions.

conservative Someone who believes that the role of government should be very limited and that individuals should be responsible for their own well-being.

Declaration of Independence The document which declared the United States free from Britain.

delegate(s) Representative(s), as to a meeting or convention.

democracy A government in which the people govern themselves through elected representatives.

dowry Money or property brought by a bride to her husband at the time of marriage.

elector(s) A member or members of a political party chosen by popular vote in each state to formally elect the president and vice president.

Electoral College The body of men and women chosen by the American voters to elect the president and vice president of the United States.

electoral votes Ballots cast by members of the Electoral College for the office of U.S. president.

emancipation The act or instance of freeing, as from slavery.

engrossed Prepared as the formal or official copy of a document or bill.

Enlightenment An eighteenth-century philosophical movement that stressed human reasoning over blind faith or obedience.

enumerated powers Those government powers itemized in the U.S. Constitution; also called expressed powers.

excise tax A tax on goods produced within a country.

faction(s) A group or groups of people with a united interest.

factionalism The existence of interest groups within a country's political parties.

federal Of or relating to a form of government in which sovereign power is divided between a central authority and a number of smaller political units, such as states or provinces.

federalist Sharing power between a national government and smaller governmental units, such as states or provinces; also, favoring a strong central government.

filibuster An attempt to expand debate upon a bill or proposal to delay or prevent its passage.

foreclosure Legal proceeding by which a borrower's rights to a mortgaged property end if the borrower fails to live up to the obligations agreed to in the loan contract.

Founder(s) Leader(s) of the thirteen colonies who established the United States of America as an independent nation.

frontier The land between settled and unsettled land.

gerrymander To divide a geographical area into voting districts to give an advantage to one party in elections.

Great Britain Island nation off the northwest coast of Europe that once ruled a worldwide empire, including the thirteen American colonies that became the United States of America.

Great Depression In U.S. history, a serious economic downturn that began with the crash of the stock market in 1929 and ended after the nation entered World War II (1939–1945) in 1941.

home rule The power of cities or local governments to govern themselves.

House of Representatives The lower house of the U.S. Congress.

impeach To formally accuse a public official of misconduct.

implied powers The powers of Congress that are not specifically spelled out in the U.S. Constitution but are deemed necessary to carry out the expressed, or specific, powers of Congress.

incumbent The holder of an office.

injunction A court order prohibiting a party from a specific course of action.

integration The mixing of different groups, especially in regard to race.

judicial review The power of a court to review laws.

legislature The branch of government that makes the laws.

literacy test(s) Exam or exams given to determine how well educated an individual is.

militia A group of citizens organized for military service; usually every able-bodied adult male.

monarchy A nation ruled by a king or queen.

monopoly Exclusive ownership of a particular good or market.

natural rights Those rights with which all individuals are born.

neutrality The policy of being neutral, or not taking sides, especially nonparticipation in war.

nullification The act by a state to declare federal laws null and void within its borders.

nullify To make ineffective.

Patriot During the American Revolution (1775–1783), one who strongly favored independence from Great Britain.

perjury The act of lying under court oath.

pocket-veto The means by which the president may kill a bill passed during the last 10 days in which Congress is in session; the president simply refuses to act on it, and the bill dies.

poll taxes Taxes paid by citizens before they vote; now illegal, poll taxes were often used to keep African Americans from voting.

popular vote Ballots cast by eligible citizens.

primary election(s) An election or elections in which qualified voters nominate or express a preference for a candidate or group of candidates for political office.

Quaker(s) A Christian religious sect that does not have a creed or clergy but believes in developing religious beliefs on inspiration from God; also called the Society of Friends.

ratification Official confirmation of a treaty or other such document by the United States Senate.

ratify To formally approve.

recession A period of declining productivity and reduced economic activity.

republican Relating to a republic, a form of government in which the people rule through elected representatives.

resolution(s) Statement(s) of issues that is relevant to only one house of Congress.

secede To withdraw from an organization.

segregation The condition of maintaining separate groups, especially in regard to race.

Senate The upper house of the U.S. Congress.

separation of powers The division of power in the federal government among the legislative, executive, and judicial branches.

separatism A belief that one group of individuals should be apart from others.

sovereignty Complete independence and self-government.

spoils system After an election, practice of the winning political party's rewarding supporters with government positions.

tariff(s) Tax on imported goods.

territory A geographical area belonging to and under the jurisdiction of a governmental authority.

unicameral Consisting of a single legislative house or chamber.

veto To refuse to approve a law.

Selected Bibliography

Adkins, Randall E., ed. *The Evolution of Political Parties, Campaigns and Elections: Landmark Documents from 1787–2008*. Washington, D.C.: CQ Press, 2008.

Aldrich, John H., ed. *Why Parties? The Origin and Transformation of Political Parties in America*. Chicago: University of Chicago Press, 1995.

Ambrose, Douglas, and Robert Martin. *The Many Faces of Alexander Hamilton: The Life and Legacy of American's Most Elusive Founding Father*. New York: NYU Press, 2007.

American Government at Work, Volume 1: The Federal Legislative Branch. Danbury, Conn.: Grolier/Scholastic Library, 2001.

Barron, Rachel Stiffler. *Richard Nixon: American Politician*. Greenboro, N.C.: Morgan Reynolds Publishing, 2004.

Bartlett, Irving H. *John C. Calhoun: A Biography*. New York: W.W. Norton, 1994.

Behrman, Carol H. *Thomas Jefferson*. Minneapolis, Minn.: Lerner Publications, 2004.

Berkin, Carol. *A Brilliant Solution: Inventing the American Constitution*. New York: Harvest Books, 2003.

Bernstein, R.B. *Thomas Jefferson*. New York: Oxford University Press, 2005.

Black, Conrad. *Richard M. Nixon: A Life in Full*. New York: PublicAffairs Books, 2007.

Boller, Paul F., Jr. *Presidential Campaigns*. New York: Oxford University Press, 1984.

——. *Presidential Inaugurations*. New York: Harcourt, 2001.

Branch, Taylor. *Pillar of Fire: America in the King Years, 1963–1965*. New York: Simon & Schuster, 1999.

Brands, H.W. *Andrew Jackson: His Life and Times*. New York: Anchor Books, 2006.

Brookhiser, Richard. *Alexander Hamilton, American*. New York: Free Press, 2000.

——. *Founding Father*. New York: Free Press, 1996.

Burgan, Michael. *Shays' Rebellion*. Minneapolis, Minn.: Compass Point Books, 2008.

Burstein, Andrew. *The Passions of Andrew Jackson*. New York: Knopf, 2003.

Calkhoven, Laurie. *George Washington: An American Life*. New York: Sterling Books, 2007.

Collier, Christopher. *Decision in Philadelphia: The Constitutional Convention of 1787*. New York: Ballantine Books, 2007.

Cox, Thomas H. *Gibbons v. Ogden, Law, and Society in the Early Republic*. Athens: Ohio University Press, 2009.

Dougherty, Keith L. *Collective Action Under the Articles of Confederation*. West Nyack, N.Y.: Cambridge University Press, 2006.

Drake, Frederick D., and Lynn R. Nelson, eds. *States' Rights and American Federalism: A Documentary History*. Westport, Conn.: Greenwood Press, 1999.

Evernden, Margery. *Wilderness Boy*. Pittsburgh, Pa.: University of Pittsburgh Press, 2001.

Feeley, Malcolm, and Edward Rubin. *Federalism: Political Identity and Tragic Compromise*. Ann Arbor: University of Michigan Press, 2008.

Feinberg, Barbara. *The Articles of Confederation*. Minneapolis, Minn.: Twenty-first Century Books, 2002.

Finlayson, Reggie. *We Shall Overcome: The History of the American Civil Rights Movement*. Minneapolis, Minn.: Lerner Books, 2002.

Fleming, Thomas. *Ben Franklin: Inventing America*. New York: Sterling Press, 2007.

Genovese, Michael A., and Lori Cox Han. *Encyclopedia of American Government and Civics*. New York: Facts On File, 2008.

Gerston, Larry N. *American Federalism: A Concise Introduction*. New York: M.E. Sharpe, 2007.

Hamilton, Alexander, James Madison, and John Jay. Edited by Clinton Rossiter. *The Federalist Papers*. New York: Signet Classics, 2003.

Hardy, Sheila Jackson, and P. Stephen Hardy. *Extraordinary People of the Civil Rights Movement*. New York: Children's Press, 2007.

Hartman, Gary L., Roy M. Mersky, and Cindy L. Tate. *Landmark Supreme Court Cases: The Most Influential Decisions of the Supreme Court of the United States*. New York: Checkmark Books, 2006.

Harvey, Bonnie C. *Daniel Webster: Liberty and Union, Now and Forever*. Berkeley Heights, N.J.: Enslow Publishers, 2001.

Hayes, Kevin J. *The Road to Monticello: The Life and Mind of Thomas Jefferson*. New York: Oxford University Press, 2008.

Hewson, Martha S. *The Electoral College*. New York: Chelsea House, 2002.

Hickok, Eugene W. *Why States? The Challenge of Federalism*. Westminster, Md.: Heritage Books, 2007.

Hogeland, William. *The Whiskey Rebellion: George Washington, Alexander Hamilton, and the Frontier Rebels Who Challenged America's Newfound Sovereignty*. New York: Scribner, 2006.

Hudson, David L., Jr. *The Bill of Rights: The First Ten Amendments of the Constitution*. Berkeley Heights, N.J.: Enslow Publishers, 2002.

Johnson, Paul. *George Washington: The Founding Father*. New York: HarperCollins, 2005.

Jones, Veda Boyd. *Thomas Jefferson: Author of the Declaration of Independence*. New York: Chelsea House, 2000.

Karmis, Dimitrios, and Wayne Norman. *Theories of Federalism*. New York: Palgrave Macmillan, 2005.

Keyssar, Alexander. *The Right to Vote: The Contested History of Democracy in the United States*. New York: Basic Books, 2000.

Kluge, Dave. *The People's Guide to the United States Constitution*. Glendale, Calif.: Action Publishing, 2007.

Levinson, Isabel Simone. *Gibbons v. Ogden: Controlling Trade Between States*. Berkeley Heights, N.J.: Enslow, 1999.

Library of Congress. "The Federalist Papers." Available Online. URL: http://thomas.loc.gov/home/histdox/fedpapers.html

Madison, James, Edward J. Larson, and Michael P. Winship. *The Constitutional Convention: A Narrative from the Notes of James Madison*. New York: Modern Library, 2005.

Marrin, Albert. *Old Hickory: Andrew Jackson and the American People*. New York: Dutton Juvenile, 2004.

Mayer, Henry. *A Son of Thunder: Patrick Henry and the American Republic*. Jackson, Tenn.: Grove Press, 2001.

McCulloch, David. *John Adams*. New York: Simon & Schuster, 2008.

Meacham, Jon. *American Lion: Andrew Jackson in the White House*. New York: Random House, 2008.

Morris-Lipsman, Arlene. *Presidential Races: The Battle for Power in the United States*. Minneapolis, Minn.: Twenty-first Century Books, 2007.

Morton, Joseph C. *Shapers of the Great Debate at the Constitutional Conven-*

tion of 1787: A Biographical Dictionary. Westport, Conn.: Greenwood Press, 2005.

Patrick, John J. *The Bill of Rights: A History in Documents.* New York: Oxford University Press, 2003.

Rakove, Jack N. *The Beginnings of National Politics.* New York: Knopf, 1979.

Rebman, Renee C. *The Articles of Confederation.* Minneapolis, Minn.: Compass Point, 2006.

Remini, Robert V. *Andrew Jackson.* New York: Palgrave Macmillan, 2008.

——. *Daniel Webster: The Man and His Time.* New York: W.W. Norton & Company, 1997.

——. *Henry Clay: Statesman for the Union.* New York: W.W. Norton & Company, 1993.

Richards, Leonard L. *Shays's Rebellion: The American Revolution's Final Battle.* Philadelphia: University of Pennsylvania Press, 2002.

Roberts, Jeremy. *James Madison.* Minneapolis, Minn.: Lerner Publications, 2004.

Schlesinger, Arthur M., Jr. *The Age of Jackson.* Old Saybrook, Conn., Konecky & Konecky, 1971.

Schulman, Bruce J., ed. *Student's Guide to Elections.* Washington, D.C.: CQ Press, 2008.

Shannon, Timothy J. *Indians and Colonists at the Crossroads of Empire: The Albany Congress of 1754.* Ithaca, N.Y.: Cornell University Press, 2002.

Simon, James F. *What Kind of Nation: Thomas Jefferson, John Marshall, and the Epic Struggle to Create a United States.* New York: Simon & Schuster, 2003.

Smith, Rick. *Ninth and Tenth Amendments: The Right to More Rights.* Edina, Minn.: ABDO and Daughters, 2007.

Sunstein, Cass R. *A Constitution of Many Minds: Why the Constitution Doesn't Mean What It Meant Before.* Princeton, N.J.: Princeton University Press, 2009.

Thompson, C. Bradley. *John Adams & the Spirit of Liberty.* Lawrence: University Press of Kansas, 2002.

U.S. Government. "Official Information and Services." Available Online. URL: http://www.usa.gov/Agencies/federal.shtml

Vaughan, David J. *Give Me Liberty: The Uncompromising Statesmanship of Patrick Henry.* Nashville, Tenn.: Cumberland House Publishing, 2002.

Watkins, William. *Reclaiming the American Revolution: The Kentucky and Virginia Resolutions and Their Legacy.* New York: Palgrave Macmillan, 2008.

White House, The. "George Washington." Available online. URL: http://www.whitehouse.gov/about/presidents/georgewashington/

——. "James Madison." Available online. URL: http://www.whitehouse.gov/about/presidents/jamesmadison/

——. "John Adams." Available online. URL: http://www.whitehouse.gov/about/presidents/johnadams/

——. "Thomas Jefferson." Available online. URL: http://www.whitehouse.gov/about/presidents/thomasjefferson/

Williams, Juan. *Eyes on the Prize: America's Civil Rights Years, 1954–1965.* New York: Penguin Books, 1988.

Witcover, Jules. *Party of the People.* New York: Random House, 2003.

Index

Page numbers in **boldface** indicate topics covered in depth in the A to Z section of the book.